It Has Its Charms . . .

It Has Its Charms...

Charles W. Morton

J. B. Lippincott Company

PHILADELPHIA and NEW YORK

Printed in the United States of America

Library of Congress Catalog Card Number: 66–23246

The author wishes to thank the Atlantic Monthly for permission to use material that originally appeared in its pages.

DESIGNED BY WILLIAM GRAY

For Mildred of the lovely, steady gaze

Contents

"What a Devil of a profession! But it has its charms . . ."
—*Voltaire*

PART ONE

●●●

Omaha, Nebraska

HOME, as nearly as I can judge it some sixty years later, was divided about equally into three parts: family, school, and summers. Geographically, home was Omaha, Nebraska, a much rawer frontier city at the turn of the century than it chose to think itself. It never occurred to me that we could or should live anywhere else, or that our manner of living was at all different from that of families everywhere. True, there were families in Omaha who lived far more splendidly than we did, who lived in big houses and kept their own horses and were driven to church of a Sunday by their own coachmen in gleaming carriages, open or closed, according to the weather, while we used trolley cars during the week and went for our Sunday drive in vehicles hired from Gorman's Livery Stable, on Leavenworth Street, just below 28th. Equally true, there were children who came to school in ragged overalls and strange, foreign-looking outer clothing in the wintertime; children who were dirty and a few—whom we regarded with curiosity and some awe—who consistently stank, quite strongly and, oddly enough, quite differently, one from another. But these variables meant nothing at all to us as schoolchildren; in fact, we were solidly instructed, at home as well as in school, that money or clothes or family had no bearing on our individual worth as Americans: all we had to do was to study hard, mind our manners, and thus prepare ourselves for the great things which would inevitably fall to us in consequence.

National origins were likewise to be ignored, and this could hardly have been otherwise in a community so filled with first-generation immigrants—Scandinavians, Poles, Bohemians, Germans, Anglo-Saxons—that it would have been impossible to envision any preferred group. We took for granted such names as Swoboda, Ruszika, Kuehne, Hostettler, Sjoberg, Gustafson, Spiesburger, Reznicek, Dowling, Rourke, Cohn, Berquist, and such. I do not recall any Negro in my class at Park School, but I believe race would have received the same indifference as religion: a private affair and of interest to nobody else. The preachment was put to us daily that religious discrimination in benighted Europe had caused the forebears of all of us to seek out the New World and to settle in the very heart of it— Nebraska. Here, whatever one's religion might be, it was his by choice and not compulsion, and we must never forget that freedom of choice was the great principle on which we should always live.

The acceptance of these ideas by the children of Park School was total, and I have often tried to account for the immense authority and prestige which the teachers enjoyed in propounding them, and indeed in asserting anything else, from the sounds of the alphabet to the multiplication table. The teacher was a person set apart and distinctly above, incapable of error, always to be believed and obeyed, the natural source of knowledge. I do not recall any child being rude to the teacher, no matter what other misbehavior might have occurred in the classroom. It would have been insufficient to say that we were docile or tractable; we were a devoted band of scholars, disciples following a stern mistress. When the fourth-grade teacher, a Miss Stapenhorst, left us to become a bride, we wept openly. I think the feeling was that here we were, just coming to grips with the rudiments of English grammar, and how could we ever expect to master them without the all-wise (and beautiful) Miss Stapenhorst?

The general climate of an Omaha public school, then, was one of hard work, carried on with great seriousness. Classes were large, thirty or more children in a single room and taught in all subjects by a single teacher; yet, as a reasonably bright boy with a fairly large and early reading background, I had all I could do to keep abreast of the rest of the class. I worked hard, and so did everyone else. The main reason, underlying what might seem today a phenomenal state of affairs, was, I believe, quite simple.

At least half the children were first-generation Americans; their parents had known only too bitterly the poverty, and the consequent lack of education, in Europe. Now laid before them was not only a free education but the same free education that all other American children would get, rich and poor alike, and the child was going to get it, and get it for all it was worth, or the immigrant parents would deal with the child accordingly. The pressure of home and school combined was irresistible, for along with the yearning for their children's advancement, these parents brought the traditional respect of the European for the teacher, the learned person.

I have no idea what traumas my classmates—or for that matter I myself—may have suffered in so hard-driving and competitive an interval. Perhaps some innate talents among us failed of disclosure by a process that was nothing more nor less than the three R's; yet many of my classmates grew up to become influential members of the community, and to me all subsequent classroom experiences seemed light exercise in comparison with the obligations imposed by the public schools of Omaha, Nebraska.

15

I make some point of the egalitarian spirit of the school, since it carried over into our after-school play and most of our social exchanges. If we inclined to make up our games and friendships from within the neighborhood, on account of mere accessibility, the only ruling standard was congeniality, and it did not matter who a child's parents were, or what he wore, or what he lived in: granted any mutual liking at all, he was welcome, fully equal, and indeed superior if he had the qualities to make him so.

So it was that a good cross-section of us went to the same dancing school, went with our parents to the Orpheum on Friday nights (no school, so sleep late the next morning), and occasionally to the Boyd Theater to savor what had been a Broadway hit only a year or two earlier.

The dancing school was conducted by a Mr. Chambers in a sizable ballroom in the basement of a building at 25th and Farnam Streets. His daughter, Halcyon, assisted him in our instruction and, as I recall her, was very nearly as proficient as Fred and Adele Astaire, the star pupils of the class, no older than we were, friendly and attractive, but so fantastically accomplished as to seem more a part of the adult world than of ours. Mr. Chambers, a slim, graying man with tightly curly hair, always gave off a powerful aroma of cloves; as my mother said darkly of him: he Drinks. Even so, he taught us the two-step, the waltz, the schottische (which remains to me only as a name), and the elements of a stilted ballroom etiquette, but for good measure we plugged away, also, at reels and "fancy dancing"; this took us through clog dancing and what we were assured were the traditional national dances of various lands— Spain, Holland, Scotland, Ireland—to appropriate piano accompaniments. The only two that I could ever get through from start to finish were the Dutch wooden-shoe bit and a "rube" dance to the tune of "Reuben, Reuben, I've Been Thinking," the first with hands on hips and a certain amount

16

of jump-ups and heel-clacking, and the latter's comic overtones supplied by a deadpan, hands-in-the-pockets routine. I cannot fairly say that I ever drew heavily on this repertory in later life, but there have been occasions when, in liquor, I have obliged with a stylized hornpipe or a double-shuffle and buck-and-wing.

Friday nights at the Orpheum gave us eight or ten years of big-time vaudeville, which afforded during its heyday a representative sampling of the entertainment world. They were the only outings of that sort to which my father would condescend; we always had the same seats—my father, my mother, and my sister who was three years my senior and ruled most of our joint doings with an iron hand.

The program followed a rigid pattern, beginning with the emergence of the orchestra into the pit, much string-plucking, tooting, tuning, and promising sounds of making ready, after which the leader would appear, a rotund, ruddy little man, with oily black hair parted in the center, who combined the functions of conductor and first violin, nodding and turning toward various members of the orchestra as he played. I am sure they would have played just as smoothly without him, but he was a fixture, well regarded by the Orpheum audience and always greeted by solid applause. He tucked a white silk handkerchief into his collar, tapped his men to the alert with a few whacks of his bow, threw back his head and—off they all went into The Overture: Zampa, Poet and Peasant, Ballet Egyptian, Light Cavalry, Waltz of the Flowers, Under the Double Eagle, Siamese Patrol, Coppelia, a noble assortment. Our favorite was "Morning" from Peer Gynt, which the drummer enlivened as the piece warmed up by blowing all sorts of cheepings, trills, and warblings. I believe these were his own idea and not Grieg's, for my sister and I exchanged disgusted glances years later when the Boston Pops Orchestra failed to greet that same dawn with even a single twitter of bird-calling. The Orpheum conductor's name was either Huster or Schuster—Alvin Schuster, as I have it. "Little Mr. Schuster," my mother called him; she was given to diminutives, and it was always "the little egg man" or "the little man at the circulating library" or "Little Mr. Resnicek"— this last a brawny neighborhood butcher who must have weighed at least 200 pounds.

After little Mr. Schuster had taken two or three bows and graciously included his men in acceptance of the applause, the program usually began with acrobats, or a cycling act, jugglers, or wire-walking—something calling for no great mental investment by the audience, and it usually ended with an offering of the same sort, an act that could withstand an audience's settling in or groping for its wraps and overshoes preparatory to leaving. The high point of the evening was "the skit"—a one-act play spotted midway through the show and often a vehicle for some celebrated stage personality. The great chiller among all skits was *The Drums of Oudh,* a melodrama of mounting tension, played throughout to the sullen beat of offstage native drumming, which became almost imperceptibly more and more menacing and culminated in a great hullabaloo when the final charge of the loud-drumming and bloodthirsty natives was broken up by the English garrison, who produced a real honest-to-god Gatling gun and cranked out with it an ear-splitting victory that left the Orpheum Theater in a haze of black-powder smoke.

Variety was of course the essence of vaudeville; its comedians, musicians, vocalists, magicians, and playlets were as popular in the music halls of London and the provinces as they were in Omaha or the Antipodes or New York. Vaudeville was the great regional equalizer of its time, and I am still mindful of the evening when I was first on my own in New York as a schoolboy and attended the "Sunday Night Concert" at the Winter Garden. Theaters were closed on Sundays, but behind this euphemism a "sacred concert," i.e., a vaudeville performance, was permitted at the Winter Garden. Smoking was allowed, also, a racy state of theatergoing indeed, with an ashtray on the back of every seat, and my expectations were of the loftiest. But I was scandalized to find myself watching a program of acts long familiar to me in the Orpheum at home, listening to the same jokes, and seeing the supposedly sophisticated New York audience falling out of its chairs at comedy routines that had been only so-so even when they were new. My uninformed reaction to the whole evening was one of disgust: these Easterners should get on to themselves and move out where vaudeville was at least up to date, even if they couldn't smoke during the performance.

Omaha, like most Middle Western cities, was laid out in squares, the numbered streets running north and south and the streets with names, more or less perpendicular to the Missouri River, east and west. Most of its houses were of wood, economically square and thus requiring a minimum of roof and exterior surface area, and altogether without blandishment. Uptown Omaha, in short, was a succession of straight streets lined with ugly houses on meager lots, the ordinary dimensions of a lot being 50 by 135 feet, although some home-owners bought an additional adjoining lot for more room and as a hopeful long-term investment. The summer heat was unkind to lawns and flowers, but a surprisingly large number of trees shaded the older streets.

The houses became larger and more pretentious in what was called the West Farnam neighborhood, but the still newer section known as Dundee, a little farther west, had clung to the fifty-foot lot through most of its development before finally indulging itself in a few curved streets and more spacious home sites. The city and with it anything like a smooth pavement ended abruptly at Fairacres, atop the next ridge west of Dundee, and beyond lay the open rolling countryside, largely treeless save for the cottonwoods and poplars screening the small farmhouses from the fierce winds. Fairacres was the city's first neighborhood to possess houses with several acres of grounds and some variety of landscaping for each; it remained an outpost of not more than ten or a dozen houses throughout the uneasy '20s, but it has long since been leapfrogged by miles of nondescript "developments," replacing with row on row of standardized houses the cornfields of an earlier day.

For children, the great lack was anything like a water playground, a beach, a pool. West of the city on the road to Millard was a pasture through which wandered a small muddy stream. Here and there it had cut through the yellow clay soil deeply enough to provide us with a slide of six or eight feet, down the wet clay and into a shallow pool. It was only a seasonal resource, a dry gully for most of the year, but when it was wet it was prized accordingly. More dependable and more hazardous was a deep pool, below an abandoned railroad trestle, where some wayward trickle from the Missouri had collected, not far from the branch trolley line that went to East Omaha. Like that of the parent river, the water here was the color of rich *café au lait,* but that was true of most natural swimming holes of the region. What finally estranged us from the place was the arrival of a middle-aged citizen one day who stripped on the trestle, produced a bar of yellow soap, and gave himself a bath in "our" pool, amid widening rings of suds. He then proceeded to launder, with much rubbing and rinsing, the union suit of long underwear that he had just taken off. It seemed to us too crass a use of what we had dimly counted a sporting and recreational location: the pool was only thirty or forty feet in diameter— too small for ourselves *and* the man's underwear and suds. We never went back there again. The Missouri itself had no place whatever in our lives; its banks were treacherous and its currents even more so. We rarely saw the river, except when crossing the bridge to Iowa, for its vast floodings and shifting

20

channels made it useless to all but a few duck hunters and squatters.

Downtown Omaha's shopping district, even with its office buildings, hotels, banks, and such, was in retrospect surprisingly small, some twenty-five square blocks or so, extending from 14th Street on the east to about 20th Street, and from Dodge Street at the north to Howard at the south. The buildings were utilitarian, most of them so stark and uninteresting that the eye tended to take them all in together as a harmonious whole in their uniform ugliness, without really looking at any one of them. One knew them by the enterprises they housed: Bennett's, the Bee Building, the Omaha National Bank Building, Browning & King, Drexel's shoe store, and of course J. L. Brandeis ("The Largest Department Store Between Chicago and Denver"), Benson & Thorne ("The Liliputian Bazar"), Myers & Dillon, the first drugstore in the city to serve a "Brownstone Front": chocolate sauce on chocolate ice cream with chopped nuts on top!

Some sort of boundary line seemed to obtain at 14th Street, especially at the intersection of 14th and Douglas, a rallying point and the uptown limit for a neighborhood of nickelodeons, employment agencies, cheap saloons, pawn shops, and pitchmen, thronged in fair weather by the stockhands, farmers, and itinerants whose business or holidays had brought them to town. The more prosperous ranchers and farmers stayed farther uptown at the Rome or the Castle, two hotels on a trolley line to South Omaha and its stockyards and packing houses, and one saw them of an evening occupying rows of rocking chairs on the broad sidewalks outside their lodgings.

The pitchmen always drew large and round-eyed crowds. Most dashing among them was one whose pitch was backed by an anatomical chart, lighted at night by kerosene flares, and who must have done very well selling "medicine"—a white powder—at $1 a can. It was harmless, he shouted, and to prove

21

it he would toss a pinch of it down his throat at intervals, but its effects were salutary beyond belief: "Just like yah old mother used to give the house its spring cleaning, that, friends, is what yah need and what yah get from this re-mark-a-ble Ginseng Compound." And why was ginseng so expensive? Simply this: the Chinese worshiped it as god . . . oldest civilization . . . inventors of gunpowder . . . long before Gutenberg printed with movable type . . . etc. Thanks, friends, and tomorrow you'll be thanking me. Another man, while King C. Gillette was still struggling for a place in the sun, sold great quantities of a straight razor at $1 each. Its peculiar virtue, he argued, was that its blade was *magnetized,* and to prove it he would dip the blade into a box of pins and hold the razor aloft to show clusters of pins adhering to it. His clincher was a harrowing account of the infections to be picked up in the ordinary barber shop, the worst of which began with "bumps on yah face" and eventually disclosed itself as "that dr-r-read disease, the ba-a-hba's ITCH," this last word being shouted at the peak of his oratorical register.

The Douglas Street area never seemed so sordid and forbidding as Chicago's skid row; it had, rather, a carnival atmosphere of garish lights and catchpenny entertainments, and its drunks were more likely to be asleep in their rooming houses or at tables in the back rooms of saloons than along the curb. Farther east and a bit north, between the so-called wholesale district and the river, was a red-light district covering several blocks through which we used to walk briskly as small boys, wondering what could lie behind all the mysterious rumors about the charms of the neighborhood, and not a little alarmed by the unaccountable remarks of the slatternly women sitting in the doorways or on the ramshackle porches of their crumbling houses. Our other occasional foray into a world still beyond our ken was to a matinee at the Krug, the older and lowlier of Omaha's two burlesque theaters, where for 10 cents a head we could sit in the gallery and see the latest weekly offering by one of the two major burlesque "wheels," which covered the country with their highly stylized shows, just as the Orpheum Circuit, Pantages, and others did with vaudeville. I have lost the names of most of the productions and their star performers, but I can recall distinctly "The Tailor-Made Girls" and the opening chorus of their show:

> "We . . . are the Tailor-Made Girls,
> Tiddy-boom, tiddy-boom, tiddy-boom . . ."

There was also the annual visitation by Ben Welch, for many years the reigning king of the Hebe comics; Bozo Snyder, who after affecting to pick something up from the stage and wiping his fingers on his trousers, would cry, "I'd like to know who it is in this town that spits like a quarter"; and Sliding Billy Watson and his Beef Trust, a genuinely outsize chorus line, vaunted to scale in at no less than 250 pounds apiece. When Sliding Billy's girls came to town the theater manager piled a dozen or so huge timbers on the sidewalk outside the theater with a sign: "I Have to Use These to Prop Up the Stage for Billy Watson's Beef Trust Girls."

The dirtier burlesque jokes were slightly beyond our understanding, but we could appreciate the Hebe, the Irisher, and the Low Dutch comics, the restaurant scene, the hotel bedroom scene, the bored straight man, and the widely varying degree of friskiness with which the chorus girls went about their work. Between the family Friday nights at the Orpheum and our furtive glimpses of the Krug's shows, I believe we saw most of the perennial comedy routines of the time.

Public gambling houses were a commonplace throughout the years that I lived in Omaha. A teen-ager could shoot craps in a rather sedate game in the basement of a cigar store at 19th and Douglas, but with a $1 minimum and a $50 maximum, plus the standard edge for the house, the game did little enough for a customer even if he seemed for a time to be hot. The currency

23

of the game was silver dollars and $5 bills or larger, all $1 and $2 bills being stuffed into a box and replaced with silver. The best thing about the game was the chatter of the stickman, whose flow of dice-table Americana compared favorably with the best of the Douglas Street pitchmen.

Farther downtown were two or three larger places which offered craps, blackjack, and chuckaluck in one room and drinks and dance-hall girls in another. There, places were heavily entrenched and well connected, as may be gathered from an incident that I place around 1916 or thereabouts, affecting one Charles W. Savage, a publicity-hunting, hell-fire preacher known as the Marrying Parson, who boasted that he had married more couples than all the other clergy in town put together, and who was affably in the press each time he tied a new knot.

A furious Prohibitionist as well as a crusading moralist, Pastor Savage was reported in the papers one day as planning a one-man descent on the more notorious establishments east of 14th Street. He was in his sixties at the time, a frail, disagreeable little man, dressed in black with a black string tie, and his proclamation was that if the police wouldn't do it, he himself would put these places out of business.

Shortly afterward, a very brief news story described the beginning and abrupt end of the Marrying Parson's ill-starred campaign. The bouncer—it was either at a place called Wick & Moore's or another with a name something like The Midway—had simply picked him up, flung him through the door and out onto the sidewalk, whence he was carted off to the hospital with a broken arm and a broken collarbone. End of story. I cannot recall that even a remonstrance with the bouncer or his employers followed, and the general feeling seemed to be that Pastor Savage would do well to stick to his knot-tying and damn well keep away from places where he wasn't wanted.

●●●

Family Interlude

BY AROUND 1908 the transition from horse-drawn vehicles was scarcely begun. The automobile was still for recreational purposes, and each new make that we saw—and there were hundreds of different ones on the streets, even in a small city like Omaha—received our closest scrutiny. A ride in any self-propelled car was exhilarating; each had its own distinctive smells and sounds; but our own Sunday afternoon "drive" was still in a surrey from Gorman's, which limited severely the range of our travels. Our usual route was via "The Boulevard," which led in a southeasterly direction to a long bridge across the railroad yards known as "The Viaduct." Here we would pause to rest the horses, while my sister and I could watch the trains—a magic word—perhaps only a switch engine or two shifting freight and cattle cars, but sometimes a big double-header freight, with a booster engine behind the caboose, or a long passenger train, bound for Denver or Billings or Cheyenne—my father usually knew where. At the far end of The Viaduct was one of the city's three principal breweries, and here we always stopped at a loading platform where a man in a leather apron brought out foaming glasses of beer for my parents. We then drove smartly home, for the livery-stable horses were always keener on the return than on the way out, while my father tipped his derby hat and exchanged bows with most of the other drivers on The Boulevard.

The parking lot of that period was the livery stable, and there were big stables and blacksmiths' shops downtown as well as in the residential neighborhoods. Farmers who had come to town only for the day in their heavy unsprung wagons hitched their big teams along the curb. The only springs in such a rig were under the driver's seat, where in bad weather the farmer, wearing a buffalo-skin coat and swathed in buffalo robes, tried to keep warm but occasionally had to clamber down and walk beside the team to get his circulation back. The ranchers and some of the farmers wore ankle-length beaver coats, sometimes with beaver lining as well, a warm, impossibly heavy garment and relatively inexpensive, for the beavers were regarded as a nuisance in the cattle country and I believe there was at one time even a bounty on them.

Of all the horse-drawn vehicles, the most sinister and the most fascinating to us was the "deadanimal-wagon," very wide, with high wooden sides, its bed so low as barely to clear the ground, which went about on call to haul away any horse that had died on the street. Our greatest interest was to find out whether the wagon was empty or horrifyingly loaded, which we could do by rushing out and having a quick peek through the crack in its tailgate. Not even a dog so compelled our sympathy as did the horse, and the sight of a dead horse on the street, or a glimpse of it in the deadanimal-wagon brought small children to the point of tears.

My mother, in a wonderfully non-interfering way, was a constantly reassuring presence. She was the conciliator in the disputes resulting from my occasional mutinies against my sister's rule, and she allowed us great freedom in deciding for ourselves what we did or did not wish to think and do. She disliked the

Omaha climate, and she found little to interest her in the city's resources, so that most of her free time she spent in reading.

Our household, during my childhood, was a good place for anyone who liked to read. We had all the standard magazines, a flow of books from the libraries, and my parents bought us great quantities of children's books. My mother was most obliging in reading aloud to me and helping me to learn to read. By the time I could read a primer in the first grade, I was considerably beyond its style and subject matter, and on learning more about how to read, I discovered that I could read for myself at a rate much faster than a person reading aloud. This was of course a real emancipation: I could read whatever I wished, at my own tempo, and if I found it tiresome I could try something else. More often than not, I was out of books and was driven to re-reading old favorites.

My reading was undirected and unrestricted, save for the nickel weeklies such as Diamond Dick, Young Wild West, Nicholas Carter, the only reading my mother forbade, unaware that their flamboyant covers contained the most fantastically moralistic literature of its time. The annual bound copy of the English children's magazine *Chatterbox*, with its dolorous woodcuts of St. Bernards hauling drowning children from skating ponds, was read and reread, as were the current volume of the *Motor Boys*, the *Dave Porter* series, or at an earlier day the fantasies of L. Frank Baum and the *Billy Whiskers* books, these last providing enough anthropomorphism to last the rest of one's life. We read all the mythological yarns, Greek, Roman, Norse, and very horrifying most of these were; we read Andrew Lang, Howard Pyle, Frances Hodgson Burnett, Joel Chandler Harris, the *St. Nicholas* with its plethora of contests and prizes, and the ghastly fairy tales of the Germans. When there was nothing else at hand I read my sister's books, *When Patty Went to College, Patty's Motor Car* (it was an electric that she won in a prize contest of some sort), the *Little Colonel* series,

27

The Five Little Peppers. We had *A Child's History of* . . . everything under the sun.

My own reading requirements were simple enough: in nonfiction a book had to deal with something of interest to me; fiction had only to be believable. This last by no means excluded the fantasy, but it did require the author to account for his tale convincingly. I could never read *Little Lord Fauntleroy* because I could never believe that any boy worth reading about would carry on the conversational fol-de-rol that he did with his mother.

It would be hard for me to exaggerate the staunchness of my mother's endorsement of us, a thick-and-thin position which she held imperturbably and without regard to what others thought of us. The complaint that we were "spoiled" she took with good-humored indifference, but in more serious issues she was a formidable defender. One of my guiltiest recollections concerns a neighbor whose house, a block from ours, we passed on the way to school. A long picket fence fronted the place and from a position safely behind the fence an aging, portly, and insanely disagreeable fox terrier screeched and snarled at every passer-by, child or adult. It was the sort of dog that brings a postman to a state of nerves, and if a child walking past happened to run a stick along the fence pickets the animal went into an ecstasy of rage.

I was about seven years old on this occasion, running my stick along the fence and finding the fox terrier in full voice, when an upstairs window was raised and a woman leaned out. She had moved too quickly to put anything more on, and she was wearing a corset and, with a tendency to bulge out of it, a corset cover. She began shouting at us. It would have been easy to dissuade us more affably, I feel certain, but her anger was almost as provocative as her dog's.

I was moved to reply. "Shut up, *fat!*" I shouted. The window went down, slam.

28

My sister and I and our constant companion Ed Dowling, who lived a block away, were summoned to the principal's office at the Park School the next afternoon. The teachers were, as I have said, respected by the children, but Miss Eveleth, the principal, was an awesome power, invoked only in grave situations. She gave us a stern account of our sins, and bade us accompany her to the offended neighbor and apologize then and there. It was a trying experience, and I am sure we must have presented a woebegone appearance to my mother, when Miss Eveleth brought us home, perhaps an hour after our usual time.

My mother said she had been worried about our nonappearance. Miss Eveleth intended, I suppose, to make sure that our parents were fully apprised of our conduct. "I am afraid this is a sad little party," Miss Eveleth began, and she went on through the whole grisly tale.

I cannot recall ever seeing my mother discountenanced, least of all by anything to do with my sister and me. She waited until Miss Eveleth completed her story. I remember being astonished by the potency of the defense my mother brought to bear in our behalf. Her manner was glacial: the principal had erred, she had made a serious mistake in not bringing us home and consulting my mother before forcing us to apologize to this woman, a family whose name my mother did not know; this was a highhanded action and inexcusable. As to the merits of the case itself, the dog was a notorious nuisance in the neighborhood and annoyed the children, making our walk to school and back a hardship, if not dangerous. As for women who shouted at small children, my mother felt comment was unnecessary. She would consult my father that evening as to what further action she might wish to take. Good afternoon, Miss Eveleth.

The episode became something of a family joke, but my mother never forgot Miss Eveleth's behavior. " 'A *sad little party*,' indeed," she would say indignantly, repeating the words of the misguided principal. "The very idea!"

My mother once took me on a small shopping tour in a light buggy provided by Gorman's. The horse was named Frank (our Sunday team were named Maude and Cob); he had a somewhat lumbering gait and interfered badly. I was about six years old and allowed to "drive" by holding the ends of the reins, below my mother's grasp of them; but this time, through an excess of trust in poky old Frank, I was allowed to drive in reality. Frank was clattering away down a slight grade when he got tangled up with himself and down he went, sliding to a stop but leaving the buggy and ourselves unharmed.

I was sure that Frank had fallen on account of some driving lapse of mine, and when I got out and saw his bright red blood on the pavement, I burst into roars of grief. Huddled with his legs every which way, Frank showed no disposition to stand up. He seemed to me to be dying and I felt that I had killed him. My mother was having none of this: she was disgusted with Frank, who got to his feet once again when my mother gave a tug on his bridle, while a helpful passerby gave him a smart kick in the rump. Frank, it transpired, had only skinned his knee, but I was saddened for days by the recollection of his wound.

More exciting even than the deadanimal-wagon was the occasional procession through the neighborhood of "movers," a word which, in this connection, I have never encountered elsewhere. There would be an ecstatic shout, "Here come some *movers*," as they passed along our street on their way somewhere else. They were, I suppose, failed homesteaders, or about to fail again as homesteaders or farmers: a procession, single file, headed by a boy of perhaps our own age mounted on a fractious-looking stockhorse, followed by a decrepit wagon or two, sagging under a load of beaten-up household effects, bedsprings, washboilers, chairs, and pathetic sundries; a surrey drawn by one or two horses and driven in rather a proprietary way by the father, head of the family, with the elder females,

30

surrounded by more belongings, in the rear seat. Perhaps there would be another wagon, driven by a suntanned girl no older than ourselves, two or three dogs trotting alongside and fully capable of standing off any nonsense from our neighborhood pets, several young horses running loose (which the movers were whispered to have stolen), and another boy of school age bringing up the rear, sometimes a boy riding bareback, simply for lack of a saddle, but impressing us with his disdainful mastery of his mount. For our part we stood at the curb gaping, marveling at the responsibilities assumed by the movers' children, wondering where they would sleep that night, and hoping that some such portion of high adventure might one day be ours. We were far beneath the notice of the movers' children, who rode by with never so much as a wave of the hand. Occasionally there were Indians who came along in outfits even more bedraggled than those of the movers, and one saw Indians downtown at times; but for the most part Indians were seen only in the waiting rooms of doctors' offices, sitting stolidly in a cloud of body odors so heavy as to seem almost visible and seeking relief from their endemic disease, trachoma.

My father's parents came to this country from England as a young couple in the 1850's. I believe their home had been in Chester or Bedford—I really do not know which—and that they were simply seeking something more than the status of a small tradesman, which would have been my grandfather's in the British class system. The senior member of the family who remained in England was one Frank Morton, my father's first cousin, who became the treasurer of a well-known firm of silversmiths. My father corresponded with him regularly for many years and regarded him as having achieved considerable success. I never did attempt to meet any of our British relatives over the years, for it seemed to me inevitable that we should disappoint each other: there were simply too many aspects of my own life that no reasonable Englishman, of whatever status or position in the world, could comfortably fit into his own categories, and I did not propose to try to account for them.

Like many other immigrants, my grandfather believed that New York had already gone through its period of prosperous expansion, and that the great future lay in the Middle West, the center of the continent, and obviously along such a natural shipping route as the Mississippi River. He settled in Burlington, Iowa, a quiet little river town, which incidentally was much the same a century later as it was when he first went there. The hard times of the 70's wiped out the hardware business he established, and in 1882 my father, who had been working for the Burlington Railroad in Lincoln, joined him in opening a hardware store in another metropolis of the future, Omaha, on the west bank of another great natural highway of commerce, the Missouri. This business, James Morton & Son Company, proved to be moderately prosperous. We were, I suppose, in the middle or upper middle income group of the community. We never had enough money, for I am sure we all spent eagerly and freely everything that came in, a practice that I have followed throughout my life. In fact, as I write these lines I estimate my net worth to be about $500 in the red; yet I live fairly well and in the comfortable belief that I can raise as much money as I need whenever I have to. It often puzzles me to reflect on the piffling plus or minus figure of my balance sheet after so many years of mistakes, carelessness, and indiscretions in money matters; but I believe many of the anxieties on this score are self-generated and needless. I have never added up a bank statement, simply because I know, and I am sure the bank knows, that my checking account is too active and too lightly upholstered to tolerate any errors or monkeyshines on the bank's part.

My parents were in their forties by the time I was born, and my grandparents died before I was five. I remember the grandparents only as austere, reserved people, my grandmother in a black dress, a small white apron, with many layers of white linen petticoats and a tiny lace cap, my grandfather in a stiff-bosomed white shirt and a black bow tie, his suit of heavy black broadcloth. They lived in a small Victorian-style brick house, painted a dun color, with narrow arched Gothic windows and with some gingerbread along the eaves, in a large yard with a fence around it, on the north side of Chicago Street between 18th and 19th Streets. They were devout Episcopalians, a commitment which the rest of my family allowed to die quietly of inanition when I was about seven years old; and since they were strict sabbatarians a Sunday dinner at their home was decidedly dull and stuffy: no games, no horseplay, children should be seen, etc. Their house could have qualified as an unobtrusive eyesore in almost any English suburb: ugly, stand-offish, primly kept, and surprisingly gloomy.

The turnover among the conspicuously well-to-do families in Omaha must have been more or less constant, although as a small boy I regarded them as immutable. A whole generation of them was brushed aside in the late '20s, when the beginnings of the Depression in the Middle West were running a year or two ahead of that trend in the East. My father took a good-humoredly cynical view of the city's big spenders, some of whom were solidly established and prepared to last out any kind of uncertainties, but many others—the grain speculators, absentee ranch-owners, financial innovators, promoters—proved vulnerable to even the light preambles to eventual disaster. The worst negative that my father would apply to any of these people was to call a man "a sport." He never succeeded in explaining precisely what the word denoted, but it implied mainly an excess of gambling—the markets, cards, or horses—and a style of clothes that he thought too flashy. A sport, in his estimation, was a short-lived entity whose preoccupations and interim successes were not worth thinking about.

One of the more picturesque "sports," unabashed and quite insistently so, was an elderly saloon-keeper named Tuthill, whose place of business, Tuthill's Tuxedo, was tucked away in an alley, directly opposite the rear entrances of James Morton & Son Company. "Tut" was tall, paunchy, white-haired; his stiff "wing" collar disclosed loose flesh like a turkey gobbler's wattles below his chin. He wore a diamond stickpin and ring of impressive dimensions, and I remember him as one of the few Omaha men with enough sense of comfort to wear cotton suits in hot weather. From his heavy watch chain, perhaps against the background of a double-breasted linen vest, hung an ivory figure of a trotting horse. My mother thought poorly of Tuthill and his place, but I was treated to an occasional lemonade from his bar and once to an unforgettably luscious sandwich of smoking hot, juicy brisket of fresh beef. In what my father called the old days, Tut's had offered a variety of gambling games, but it was only a saloon in later times. I think it fair to say that practically all the big business transacted by James Morton & Son Company was clinched at the bar of Tuthill's Tuxedo: if an important customer came in, my father took him across the alley to Tut's while the salesmen from the Eastern manufacturers always took my father and the buyers there. My mother's annoyance with Tut's came from trying to reach my father by telephone during his short business day, only to hear, "Sorry, but he's just stepped out." My father was never beholden to alcohol, but our chief buyer, a witty Scotsman, found it an occupational illness and would vanish every so often for a sojourn in a Keeley Cure.

I mention my father's business day as short, which it was, in point of ordinary business hours. But it began with his getting up around 4:30 A.M. and taking "the first car"—the first trolley of the day—at a corner near our house, a few minutes after five o'clock. He reached the store some fifteen minutes later, let himself in, and spent the next two hours in pricing all the items listed in the "day book" of the previous day—a book in which the clerks and everyone else who worked in the store wrote down the precise description and quantity and the price, if at retail, of any goods charged to a customer's account. Any sale not charged was rung up in the cash register, to which all the clerks and even the delivery boys had complete access, and without any tickets or paperwork to slow things down. They all had equal access to any part of the inventory, some of which was quite valuable. The cash register might show itself to be a few dollars short or long when the bookkeeper balanced it each midafternoon, but in all my years in Omaha I never heard so much as a hint of dishonesty on the part of anyone who ever worked for my father.

With the day book priced and ready for billing, my father shaved at the lavatory—a washbasin and no more, the toilet being hidden away in the cellar among the rolls of hardware cloth and bins of machine bolts—after which he picked up his mail from Box 418 at the main post office, a half-block from the store, and ate his breakfast at a small German restaurant, Rump's, directly across the street from the store. He lunched around 11:30 at Ed Maurer's, probably the best downtown restaurant for men the city had or ever will have, and left for home at 2:30. After a bath and a nap he joined his family downstairs at around 5:00, drank two martinis made with dry gin and a spoonful of sweet Italian vermouth (a formula with which I came to concur many years later), and presided at our 5:45 P.M. dinner. By 7:30 he was in bed, reading, and his light was out an hour later. He wore linen nightshirts and was the only member of the family to insist on linen for sheets and pillow cases. His underwear was of Irish linen from Marshall Field's, with green shamrocks in the selvage.

Supplies for the household table were selected by my father at an old-fashioned downtown grocery store, Buffet's, where he spent a quarter-hour every morning in consultation with Frank

35

Buffet, its proprietor. Our meat he ordered twice a week from Cudahy's retail market in South Omaha. I doubt that any family in the city was more fastidiously provided for, although my father ate sparingly, always in portions so small as to invite chaffing him, especially in view of the hubbub he raised over anything not properly cooked. The cost of food was almost negligible among family expenses of that time, and the going wage for the diligent immigrant girls who cooked and did the housework was $4–5 a week. To forage in our refrigerator was a first-rate adventure in the cold buffet.

At some time in his twenties, before his marriage, my father made the Grand Tour of Europe and Great Britain. His findings from the Continent were meager: an antique coin of the Caesars that he wore as a watch charm; but he had been enchanted by England and Scotland, and by the splendors of the *Carmania* and the *Etruria* of the Cunard Line. This was the outing, I believe, that reinforced his enjoyment of good clothes and gave him a resolute set of standards of dress that he followed for the rest of his life. Never a man at ease with words, he had trouble in communicating to me what had most impressed him, and it usually came down to something like, "London . . . it was wonderful. You'll see for yourself some day . . ." I think I must have been fifty years old before there dawned on me the whole complexity of what he had vainly tried to describe: the pomp and grandeur of Imperial England, the rigid conventions, the homogeneity despite the class distinctions, the luxury surrounding the well-to-do traveler, the surpassing novelty of the scene as it unfolded before one newly arrived from Nebraska. I am sure, even so, that he preferred to be his own man in Omaha, to be able to move in whatever circles he chose —although he chose in fact to move in no particular circles at all. He belonged to two clubs, but rarely went to either except for a dinner with his family: the Field Club, where I played tennis and golf; and the Omaha Club, a downtown stronghold of fine cooking where I learned later on to play four-handed hearts for punishing stakes and table-stakes poker for far more money than I could afford.

When we were small and playing in the yard at home after school, we kept watching down the street for the first glimpse of my father on his walk from the trolley. He was not tall— perhaps five feet five—and with his quick, confident step he was identifiable as far as he could be seen at all. Whatever game we were playing broke up in a race to escort him home, and he was pleased and a little embarrassed at the warmth of his welcome by all hands.

Downtown he conducted his business as a one-man affair, without any real second-in-command; there was no detail of it that escaped him, and he carried in his head an astounding list of costs and selling prices, sizes, discounts, and precise data for thousands of items. There was no function in the store in which he could not engage usefully, and I can still envision him in a busy interval: in shirt sleeves, disclosing the elegant handiwork of Albert Cahn, the city's favored shirtmaker and the best balk-line billiard player in Omaha; tobacco-brown felt hat, carefully telescoped and pinched; a Havana cigar clenched between his teeth; lugging a keg of nails down the aisle to a waiting customer and refusing any offers of assistance. He was just as courteous to the men who worked for him as he was to everyone else. He occupied a roll-top desk in the center of the main floor, surrounded by the maximum activity that a working day could produce.

Each November my father went to Chicago to pick out our Christmas toys at Marshall Field's, and by the time I was ten he would take me with him on short business trips to New York. He ordered also his annual supply of whisky on these trips from Acker, Merrill and Condit. We lodged in New York at the Knickerbocker Hotel, shifting a few years later to the 34th Street Waldorf, which stands firmly in my mind as the most glamorous and profoundly enjoyable of any American hotel in my experience.

What impressed me first of all about the Waldorf was its vast marquee, which must have extended, at the main entrance, along perhaps a third of the building's 34th Street side, enough to shelter the occupants of eight or ten vehicles at a time and lavishly lighted by countless bulbs. At the curb were a long rank of hansom cabs, a closed carriage or two, and a sprinkling of the brass-bound, chugging taxicabs that were just coming into use. The bar, with its huge mirrors and pyramids of shimmering glasses, was equally distinguished; on each of the tables in this spacious room was an Edam cheese in impeccable condition, and it was a splendid experience to sit there with my father, munching cheese and water biscuit, drinking a Horse's Neck of Cantrell & Cochrane's pungent ginger ale, while my father drank a half-bottle of hock and we both speculated on who some of the more significant-looking customers at the bar might be. The marquee was, incidentally, the first I ever saw to carry a special panel on which the carriage starter or doorman could cause to appear in electric lights a number, and thus summon from the waiting vehicles the one to which he had assigned that number when it had first unloaded its passengers. The opera houses and even most theaters were similarly equipped, and many limousines of those days bore a distinctively colored light on the roof, to help a readier identification by the owner, especially at some distance.

The surpassing pleasure at the Waldorf was a meal across the corridor from the bar in the Men's Café, another room so vast as never to seem too crowded, paneled in oak and with oaken columns of Corinthian design towering to a coffered ceiling of elaborately carved beams. Everything here was perfection: the heavy armchairs with thick leather cushions, the crisp linen, the same elderly waiters year after year and their devout professionalism, the marvelous food, and always the aroma of a men's richly munitioned dining room, a delicate blend of cookery odors, a whiff of wine, and the smoke of good cigars. My favorite treat at the Men's Café was a pot of chocolate, which cost 35 cents and was presented in a ritualistic silver service on a silver tray: a large pot—perhaps three cups—of dark, slightly bitter chocolate; a pot of hot milk; a sugar bowl; and a long dish piled with whipped cream, flavored with a hint of vanilla and a touch of sugar and made from heavy cream and not the substance that nowadays comes spluttering out of a pressure can. It was a great dish to start the day or to fortify a lunch. Rooms at the Waldorf were luxurious, with many a fine Oriental rug to enliven the carpeting, and furniture and accessories of the most delightful quality. The whole establishment seemed designed to last, gracefully, for centuries, yet such was and is the self-devouring way of New York that the Waldorf survived only into the '20s. Its guiding genius during its heyday was, I believe, one George Boldt, and without him the hotel went into a long decline, worsened by Prohibition, in its final years. Of the present Waldorf on Park Avenue, in comparison with the hotel that made the name famous, the less said, it seems to me, the better.

Train travel fascinated the Middle Westerner; it was his only means of escape from the isolation, the savage climate, the sameness day after day of life in the farm country's small cities and towns. A Bostonian, dividing the year between his winter home and the north shore of Massachusetts Bay, might almost never need to set foot on a train, save for trundling along for an hour or so in the coaches of the Boston & Maine, with their open windows and sea breezes, or an infrequent sprint to New York. The differences between living in a city of terminals and a place that is merely on the way to one are manifold; people in Omaha counted the train travel itself as an important part of their outings; the performance of the several lines serving the city was taken with great seriousness.

My father was extraordinarily premature in meeting any commitments at a fixed time; departures on a 6:30 P.M. train found us all seated in the waiting room by four o'clock. At 5:45 we were standing at the gate in the train shed waiting for the Omaha cars, which were to be attached to the through train from the West, to be opened for passengers, which occurred a quarter-hour later. Many years later, when my wife and I returned from our first trip to Europe, my father wanted to hear all about our departure from New York on the way over. "What time did the ship sail?" he asked me.

"Three in the afternoon," I said.

"And what time did you go aboard?"

"I think it was about twelve-thirty, maybe one o'clock."

My father gave me a horrified look. "My god, Charlie . . . ," he said.

His habit of prematureness has remained with me ever since. In the summers when I was commuting from Boston to Gloucester, I was always at the gate waiting for the 4:58 to be opened, and several times I was so early that I caught the preceding train, only to have to wait in the station at Gloucester until my wife appeared to meet the 4:58. It seems as if I have spent almost as much time in stations and waiting for trains to start as I have riding on them, but I was finally outwitted by the shuttle planes between Boston and New York: they left every half-hour and there was no real way of being too early for one.

I suppose the element of great distance was exciting in train travel, and to arrive on the scheduled minute after a long overnight run seemed a wonderful feat. The ravishing example of this for a child was the moment at Englewood of a morning—sunny, snowy, rainy—when the green cars of the Chicago-bound Twentieth Century of the New York Central and the red train of the Pennsylvania's Broadway Limited miraculously pulled in together and came to a gentle stop on parallel tracks, a split-second dead heat after a fast night trip over highly dissimilar routes. The porters and waiters all seemed to know each other by name and gathered in the vestibules of each train, waving their greetings as the trains moved off together and separated for their different destinations downtown. Even more of the glamour in long-distance railroading marked the ride on the Burlington, when the train bound from Omaha to Billings stopped at the little cow town of Arvada, Wyoming, to wait for its counterpart to pass. Here the vast emptiness of the sagebrush country reached almost to the station platform, where the traveler got off for a stretch. A distant whistle sounded, and coasting down the fairly stiff grade came the train for Omaha, indeed for far-off Chicago, a curving succession of dust-covered mail cars, baggage cars, coaches, and Pullmans, the starched white jackets of the gesticulating porters and waiters showing up reassuringly against their travel-stained backgound. As the observation car passed, the handful of passengers seated on its roomy rear platform—real railroad buffs out in the dust and cinders—gave us a sophisticated wave. There being nothing else to detain a long-distance train at Arvada, ours set out again immediately to begin champing and belching its way up the hill.

Of all the grades in the days of steam I believe I preferred the Sherman Hill, just west of Cheyenne, where the Overland, Limited, with two huge locomotives up front and a freight engine for a booster at the back, all with much rail-sanding and wheel-slipping and the roar of their exhausts, managed to maintain something like a twenty-mile-an-hour pace to the summit. It was stirring after the long climb, when the booster finally dropped off and disclosed the scene behind, to look back in the deceptively thin air and see how near Cheyenne still seemed to be and how steep and abrupt was the grade that we had just overcome. One remembers fondly the long eastbound freights, with dozens of the yellow cars of the Pacific Fruit Express sandwiched among other names and colors, tearing down the slope through Big Springs, in the corner of Nebraska beyond North Platte near the Colorado line, with the glare from the open firebox flaring into the night sky. Surely the fireman must have timed his shoveling to dazzle the beholders in the little towns as the train screamed through and the rear lights of the caboose winked out in the distance.

Only once did I ever encounter the phenomenon of "the silk train," which seemed to impress the conductor and trainmen as much as it did the passengers. I was aboard a day train headed east through Iowa. Our train went into a siding, and the word was passed that we were waiting to be overtaken by a silk train —a special of three baggage cars only, carrying silk from the Orient from a West Coast port to Chicago, the silk so valuable that any hours wasted in transit meant the loss of large sums in interest charges. I do not know the truth of it, but the tension mounted as we sat there on the siding until the special rocketed by in a single whoosh, hitting along, so our conductor estimated, at 100 mph and precisely on time.

In making up a Pullman berth for the night, the porter would, on request, open the window at the foot and lower it to rest on a finely meshed brass screen, perhaps eight inches high, through which, as the night wore on, came not only the cool air of the prairies—along with a surprising quantity of cinders —but also the odors and sounds, at very close range indeed, of another feature of the Western railroads: the cattle train. One might even find his train stopped alongside a cattle train in the small hours and be roused suddenly by the bawling of the cattle, the bleats of sheep, the squealing of hogs, and with these sounds there swept in through the brass screen the pervasive and distinctive stench of too many animals too closely confined for too long. Sheep were often loaded in cars with extra decks, thus affording space for two or three layers of sheep in a single car, which, since the sides were slatted and gave plenty of ventilation, made no great difference save, perhaps, in multiplying the stench and noise they gave off. I know nothing about the cattle trains of today, but I assume they are still useful for long hauls of large numbers of animals. The stockhands accompanying the train to market used to travel in the caboose or a boxcar, but as recently as the 50's I saw in the Northwestern's yards at Council Bluffs several large, handsome cars with open, brassbound rear platforms and identified on the sides, like the name of a Pullman, as "Drovers' Car." Like the private cars of old, once the accessory of every right-thinking millionaire but now called "business cars" by the railroad executives who seem too timid to indulge in them, the Drovers' Car had an air of disuse.

The overnight change of scene, on the trains from Omaha, was always stunning. From the train to Billings one looked out the next morning on the limitless panorama of the barren country around Edgemont, South Dakota, the wind-scoured buttes that formed the end of almost every ridge, each with its sprinkling of stunted pines, edged so sharply in the clear air that it all seemed viewed through a powerful lens. In the other direction, the eastbound traveler debouched into the pandemonium of Chicago traffic, potent, violent, yet somehow orderly enough to allow the three-horse Frank Parmelee omnibus, the ticket for which was part of one's long Burlington–New York Central ticket, to rumble smartly over the cobblestones to the Lasalle Street Station. Chicago was where I first heard a traffic policeman's whistle in use—a sound that for many years conjured up for me the morning darkness of the Loop, struggling with itself under the tracks of the Elevated, the huge dray horses clawing at the pavements as they tried to set in motion again the massive wagons, the *sang-froid* of the drivers, the medley of uproar from all directions. The omnibus was comfortably upholstered in cloth, neatly kept, and accommodating fifteen or twenty passengers who sat facing each other in two seats extending fore and aft, the luggage being carried on the roof, and the driver seemed always able to keep the horses at an excitingly fast trot through the crowded streets and even around corners.

I came to know Chicago fairly well in later years. The city alarmed and fascinated me—such a corner, for instance, as 22nd and Wabash around midnight; or the back room of the Jackson Café, a neighborhood saloon on, I believe, 55th Street on the South Side; or Harry James's Place, a basement cabaret at the corner of Clark and Kinzie which served only salted nuts and drinks and not even a slice of bread or a cup of coffee, where I first heard, around 1918, the New Orleans Jazz Band and a fabulous Negro ensemble called the Louisville Jug Quartet. Harry James was unrelated, I am sure, to any later celebrities of that name, and he was the impresario of the greatest hot music I have ever heard in this country to this very day. The finest saloon of my youth was in Chicago—an L-shaped bar called Righeimer's in the Loop, where a pinkly lighted fountain splashed at the corner of the L, and a wonderfully deft Negro, elderly and benignant, made indescribably delicate ham or roast beef sandwiches—the free lunch—using only two long slicing knives and never touching either bread or meat with anything else and extending to the patron, through a window in his cubicle, the faultlessly neat sandwich held between the two blades. He was a charming man and was pleased by any compliment on his style. It was delightful, on a hot day, to stand in the airs from the ceiling fans in Righeimer's cool, quiet bar, and make a lunch of a bourbon eggnog—shaken to a perfect chill by the bartender, himself a great stylist—and two or three of the gossamer sandwiches. Righeimer's was celebrated, also, for an upstairs room that simulated a ship's cabin, where an ocean mysteriously rising and falling was seen through portholes in the wall; but the little fountain and its sounds made the street-level bar irresistible.

My father was fond of a small German restaurant in Chicago, where his friends liked to lunch, called Schimpfermann's, a dingy, hearty sort of place serving Munich beer on draught, and it was characteristic of his lifelong kindness to me that he would take me instead to Rector's, where George Rector was making his name with a large, conventional, and very good restaurant more to my liking, even though my idea of a feast as a small boy, which could have been satisfied almost anywhere but Schimpfermann's, was a large portion of spaghetti with tomato sauce.

The quality of dining-car service and meals had much to do with one's choice of routes and trains. East of Chicago, especially on the extra-fare trains, the diner was about the equivalent of a good metropolitan restaurant, with little to put any one line significantly ahead of another. My father regarded the Burlington's 6:30 train for Omaha as even better, possibly because he knew so many of the stewards and waiters by name, and on this train our procedures were unvarying: first at the gate, waiting for it to open; first aboard the train; then instantly to the dining car, where we were necessarily the first arrivals of the evening.

Serving liquor before the train left was prohibited, so my father's double martini was delivered in a teacup. We would be all but through with the meal by the time the train pulled out, and my father's beer with his dinner came in a coffee pot, with cup and saucer. Steak was no great treat to the Middle Westerner—Louis Ahko's Chinese restaurant in Omaha offered an excellent T-bone on the Business Man's 50-Cent Lunch to any who were foolish enough to prefer it over his Chinese dishes—but the aged and flavorsome beef of the Burlington, was celebrated and I suppose it would have seemed uncouth to order anything else. I did learn from my father's management of a dining-car meal the great results to be had from a thoughtful parley with the steward and a between-meals consultation with the chef in his galley, with a tip to each, particularly in regard to any meat dish in which the quality is largely determined by the cut of the individual portion—a veal cutlet, for instance, which can be anything from an important success to a knife-resisting calamity. I did learn from a dining-car steward why the hashed brown potatoes on trains were usually so far ahead of what one got in the ordinary restaurant: the reason, said he, was that the dining car of an evening usually had on hand several baked potatoes; if these were chilled for at least twelve hours, then peeled and coarsely grated, allowed to form a crust over a very slow flame in a heavy skillet and flopped once, the result had a flavor all its own that boiled potatoes would not produce. A tablespoon of olive oil will suffice for the skillet in this process, and if this were counted as the ration of fat, one finds that the potato enlarges itself so showily in the grating that a single potato will yield two portions, and the dish is by no means as inimical to a diet as might be supposed.

●●

CHAPTER THREE

Summers:
The Pleasures of the East

THE GREAT summer outings for my mother, my sister, and me began around the first of June and extended through most of September. I doubt that I ever finished a school year or began one at the appointed time; nor did I ever stay on anywhere long enough to receive any sort of diploma. Only once or twice did my father ever join us during these summers, and then only briefly; he was restless when he was away from his business for more than a few days, and I think he was always relieved to have his importunate family a half-continent away for a time. He was an affectionate correspondent, writing to my sister and me as often as he did to my mother and always enclosing in his letters to us children a small leaflet of some sort, from which fluttered a dollar or two for us to squander.

Train travel was a matter of passes during my childhood; no one of any substantial connections bought and paid for a ticket, and the cost of our transportation to the East was only the Pullman fare for a stateroom. Our passes came to us on the proposition that my father was a sufficiently large shipper of freight, and it was perfectly true that it was for him to say by what road all freight shipments to and from his business were routed, but the Interstate Commerce Commission eventually wiped out these perquisites as constituting unfair competition. The passes were not valid on the extra-fare trains; we rode an exasperatingly slow train from Chicago to Albany, where we changed for Troy, making still another change, I believe, before finding ourselves on an even slower and dirtier local for Williamstown. Soon familiar summer landmarks began to appear, and by the time we sighted the gray cobblestones of the Williamstown station we were in ecstasies. At the platform we boarded the rather battered yellow omnibus of "Charlie" Bates, who met all the trains, and were driven uptown to the Greylock Hotel, where we usually remained until the last week in July. By August, Williamstown was likely to be too hot, and we moved on to some similar establishment on the Maine coast for the rest of the summer.

My mother's older sister, Mary Turner Salter, lived in Williamstown; her husband, Sumner Salter, was the college organist and choir director; they had four children, three boys and a girl, too old for our activities with the exception of the youngest son, who was only about a year older than I was and who was our daily companion. The Salters' lives were dominated by music, my aunt being a quite successful composer of songs and her husband an arranger of some distinction. My own sister was by way of being a superb pianist, phenomenally gifted, whose piano playing I have always preferred over the years to any other; she had an incredibly long and accurate memory, could play almost anything that she ever heard, positive pitch and all that, and was fond of jolting the listener abruptly by changing to another key right in the middle of some familiar passage, the more complex and difficult the better. The Salters' house was overflowing with great stacks of music, and the sound of it was constant: my sister taking a whirl with her Czerny, or Aunt Marie working out a new song, or Uncle Sumner in a long trial-and-error session shaping an arrangement for Schirmer. Evenings, all these people would get together for solos, duets, trios, arrangements for four hands, two pianos, the moony German songs, musical-comedy successes, and everything imaginable. My sister flitted briefly in and out of a finishing school or two, but her education in everything but music really ended with the eighth grade, and she was never any great shakes intellectually. Her playing has remained throughout her life as subtle, as witty, unpredictable, original, and beguiling, as I could wish to hear. I have listened to her for uninterrupted hours, as one mood gave way to her next, only to come upon some tag or fragment that opened new vistas in still more untouched memories or sounds not previously ventured. The whole accrual of her personality finds expression through the keyboard as through nothing else.

The road between Williamstown and North Adams was the only paved highway in the vicinity; all the others were gravel, pocked with puddles after a summer rain, leading past small farms whose owners were old-time up-state types, driving buggies or pungs, according to the season, and giving off clipped witticisms with many a b'god and b'gum. Most of the roads followed brooks and streams, where about half our day was spent in fishing and swimming. We all had bicycles, and our favorite place was the Sucker Hole, three or four miles up the Cold Spring road to South Williamstown and reached just after a pause at a horse trough, where a stream of icy water emptied, after coming down a long hillside in a series of open wooden conduits. The Sucker Hole itself was a classic of its kind: a sharp bend in the stream imposed by a steep cliff of rock, whence one could plunge into six or seven feet of water that shoaled almost immediately in a gravel bottom that even a city child's bare feet found congenial. As the summers went by, we spent more and more time playing tennis, and baseball of varying orthodoxy. The whole village and countryside constituted a playground, the hay and cattle barn of a farm no less than its woods and orchards. There was also, a few miles distant and

easily reached by bicycle, a strange little spa called Sand
Springs, where for 15 cents each we could change in a bath-
house and swim—in our all-covering bathing suits—in a con-
crete pool filled with "Wampanoag Water" from the springs,
said to have great curative properties discovered by the Wampanoag Indians, and sold in elaborately labeled bottles at the
office. The same water was used in Sand Springs Ginger Ale,
which thus took on remarkable therapeutic powers as a soft
drink. Our problem was whether to spend the extra dime or
two at Sand Springs or wait until we could get the much better
value for the money at Wally Brigg's soda fountain "down-
street" as the local idiom had it for Spring Street, i.e., downtown, the only "business" district in Williamstown.

Life at the Greylock Hotel was much to my taste: a tranquil,
well-kept place, with shuttered as well as solid doors for the
bedrooms to catch the drafts on a warm night, and always a
raffish desk clerk or two who could be persuaded to sell cigarettes to me and my cousin at an outlandishly early age. The
meals were typical of the better New England summer hotel,
where the guests came to stay and not to go dusting off in a
new move every few days: practically everything the region
afforded in foodstuffs at noon and evening, after a breakfast
menu that always listed beefsteak and lamb chops in addition
to all else, and even on occasion wild strawberries.

The proprietor of the Greylock, Henry N. Teague, was a
Down-East Yankee who spoke that dialect so rapidly as to be
barely intelligible. He was just coming to grips, around 1911, with
the touring motorist, and the half-dozen pioneers who came to
Williamstown daily in this pursuit usually lunched at the
Greylock or spent the night there. The hotel had an "auto
entrance" with a high step at the front of its stair leading to
the verandah; an arrival or departure here meant a great flurry
of bellboys and chauffeurs and, not least, the intrepid tourists
themselves in their linen dusters and goggles, the ladies with

swathings of veils and the men with large driving gauntlets—not merely for show, if one recalls the exposure to rain in cars that sometimes had neither top nor windshield.

The luggage was usually wrapped in a kind of black oilcloth, as a protection against rain and dust, before being strapped on the running boards and a "trunk rack" at the rear. The vehicles themselves, at a time when a large car that could tour dependably without breaking down was only for people of considerable means, represented the cream of American and European design, scarcely any two alike, and each an object of gaping and wonderment for the small fry such as ourselves.

Tourists in their cars, then, were not only good business for Henry N. Teague but a promise of more to come in the years ahead. He had a keen sense of public relations, and it occurred to him that a bit of handshaking and exchanges of hospitality with the proprietors of other hotels like the Greylock ought to build up new revenues of this sort. He began a series of one-day trips to the better hotels nearby—the Red Lion Inn at Stockbridge, the Curtis House at Lenox, the Idlewild at South Williamstown—and, as I was watching his departure with his senior clerk one morning, he invited me to come along as a back-seat passenger. Teague was so tall and so florid that my mother referred to him as "Mr. Teague" without her customary diminutive, and she was quite willing to entrust me to his driving; so began for me a wonderful survey of summer hotels.

Teague's car was a 1911 Chalmers "30" touring car, a rather too bulky body for an absurdly short hood and too small a four-cylinder engine. I remember it particularly because the first pressure on the clutch pedal activated the clutch, while pressure more than halfway down began to apply the foot brake, leaving the right foot free at all times to use the accelerator. It was a tough little car, the model on which Chalmers-Detroit was to found its relatively ephemeral reputation for durability. Aside from the clincher tires—"fabric" tires not unlike old-style

51

garden hose in construction—which punctured easily, our travels were free from troubles. By the end of our Greylock interval in the following summer, Teague had lengthened his trips to two or three nights on the road, and I was the beneficiary of many stops in the White Mountains and Maine, and even at the awesome infinities of the Grand Union, at Saratoga Springs. Certainly, without the auspices of Henry N. Teague I should never have seen the interior of Richard Canfield's defunct gambling house at Saratoga, or experienced the marvelous hospitality of Ekwanok, at Manchester, Vermont, this last having seemed to me far and away the most charming and elegant of them all. From Ekwanok, I recall a youngish chap whose name I believe was Freddie Martin, a distinguished amateur golfer and son of the proprietor, who dined with me and answered all my questions about the hotel with the greatest urbanity while his father was playing host to Teague. I never saw Teague again in later years, but I believe he lived to a great age, always active in New England's tourist business, and when I last heard of him he was the proprietor of the cog railway on Mount Washington.

One of the great moments of a child's day at a summer hotel was when, after what seemed an interminable wait just outside, The Doors opened for dinner and there stretched the vast dining room, each table with its little vase of flowers, its caster of seasonings and oil and vinegar, and its standardized plate of little cakes to accompany other desserts. The very first summer hotel of my recollection was on Great Chebeague Island in Casco Bay; it was on a grassy hilltop, a rambling white building with the usual wide verandahs and rocking chairs; I believe it was called the Cliff House, but no matter. My sister and I were waiting—starving—for The Doors to open. I was just over four years of age, and she was seven-plus.

I should explain that the little cakes on each table were so commonplace that not even a child would bother with them in the course of a meal, and there was certainly nothing of Forbidden Fruit about them, but some wild urge into mischief overcame my sister. She opened one of The Doors a crack—in itself a breach of good conduct—beckoned me to follow, thus ensuring that the guilt would be shared, and we tiptoed into the empty room. She was wearing some frilly white dress; I was in the boy's dinner attire; a starchy white sailor suit with long trousers and a whistle on a white cord around my neck; we were both "slicked up" for the evening.

Our own table was too far into the room to risk, and I suppose there was no real challenge in stealing cakes from one's own table, but at any rate my sister reached into the cakes on a table just inside The Doors. She seized one and extended it toward me.

"Here," she commanded. "Take a bite."

I did not realize that she was holding the cake in such a way that I should have only a very small bit indeed, and I obeyed energetically, with a lunge such as I imagine a snapping turtle or a barracuda might make toward some delicacy it fancied. My jaws closed on the cake, but there was a screech from my sister as they attempted to close, also, on her thumb, with which she had been stingily conserving the much greater part of the piece for herself—in fact, I could never have dreamed that she was leading me into these fantastic risks for a fragment as small as what her thumb had calipered off for me.

My sister's screech gave way to yelling at her maximum lung power as her thumb, wrenched from my bite, bled prodigally all over everything: her, me, the tablecloth, the floor. My own outcries, as much in surprise as in horror or guilt, rose accordingly. We must have baffled the first arrivals of waitresses and guests and my mother: two bloodstained children, screaming so loudly that no one could imagine what had befallen them, as we were hustled away for repairs.

My sister wore, with an air of some virtue, a bandage on

her thumb for a week or more, and a faint scar there, incidentally, ever after. I am sure that at least some of the other
guests eyed me with misgivings for behavior so savage by one
so young.

For several years, before the great fire early in this century,
we spent the Maine part of our summer at the Seashore House,
in Old Orchard, a bourgeois resort with a "pier" and a magnificent beach, where many Middle Westerners and Canadians
came to cool off. The Seashore House, save for the big plate of
steamed clams and the cup of undiluted essence of clam broth
on the menu each evening, was much like the Greylock: the
same long verandahs and rocking chairs, the same sort of "trio"
to play dinner music and the light classics, the occasional itinerant entertainer, the Saturday night dance for the children, and
the same impression of well-being and relaxation.

The Seashore House was situated right on the sand, protected by a low wooden bulkhead only a few yards above the
long boardwalk which followed the beach at about the high-
water mark. Instead of along the streams and in the fields of
Williamstown, a child's day was spent here on the beach, most
of it in great construction projects, designed but never quite
able to withstand the incoming tide. The work was interrupted
briefly by plunges into the paralyzingly cold surf. The surf was
heavy, quite safe, and altogether enchanting; but a few minutes
of its chill would turn a child a rich plum color, barely able
to assert, teeth chattering, to the parent, "It's warm as toast."
The hotel had its own bathhouses where the guests changed,
and one remembers them for the strangely insipid taste of the
fresh-water shower after the tangy surf, the smell of the sun-
baked wood and wet bathing suit, and the sand that not even
the most persistent toweling ever quite removed from between
one's toes.

Just before dinnertime at the Seashore House each evening,

an old woman whom I recall as an Indian from a surviving fragment of some Maine tribe appeared in the lobby with a long basket of varicolored sweet peas of great size and fragrance. Before a children's party, I was allowed to buy a bouquet of these and present them to a fabulous girl of my own age, who came there each summer with her grandparents, from Burlington, Iowa, where my parents in their own early days there had known the family. I call her fabulous because she was companionable, extraordinarily pretty, and the memory of the steady, enigmatic gaze of this violet-eyed playmate remained with me throughout the rest of the year. At Christmastime I wrote her a faithful account of the presents I had received, and to see her again in the next summer was no less than a dream come true. I was her partner in leading many a Grand March at the children's parties, but the great fire wiped out the Seashore House along with everything else at Old Orchard, and we lost each other for several years in summering elsewhere. Unexpectedly, around 1913, I saw her again briefly—more beautiful, if anything, still with her lovely, steady gaze—when we were staying at Kennebunk Beach and she was with her grandparents in Kennebunkport, a few miles up the coast.

Another hiatus followed, until one evening in the fall of 1917, when, on my way back to Omaha over the road after another summer in the East, on the outside chance that she might be there, I rang the bell of her grandfather's house in Burlington, only to have her open the door to me. She was wearing a dark blue foulard dress, with a small pattern in white and a narrow white collar—piqué, I believe. She was surprised and, I thought, pleased to see me. There was never another hiatus in my relationship with her. I wrote to her almost every day for the next two years. My vehicle at the time was a 1917 Stutz, a four-passenger touring car known as the "Bulldog Special," and nothing was more exhilarating than a spring across Iowa, something over 300 miles of dirt road, in this delightful car with the expectation—thunderstorms permitting —of that evening mounting the steps of the dignified old house at 805 North Fourth Street, in Burlington. After her grandfather's death in 1918 she lived with her father in New Orleans. We were married there in 1920, just on the point of reaching age twenty-one.

●●

CHAPTER FOUR

Schoolboy's New York

I WAS TRYING one day not long ago to give a lift to a boy who was having great trouble in translating Latin. "I hate this sort of thing," he said. "It's really nothing but memory work. But in geometry and some of these other subjects you have a chance to use your mind and do some reasoning."

For his own purposes his complaint was sound enough, but he may have hit upon, at the same time, the reason for my own fondness for Latin, and to a lesser extent Greek, and my general unease in mathematics. Memory work in great blocks— poems, proclamations, chunks of Shakespeare—had been loaded on us all the way through the eighth grade. I can still rattle off lines from a history textbook on the Ordinance of 1787, though I retain nothing else of it but the mere words: "Hardly had Congress provided for the sale of the land than a number of Revolutionary soldiers formed the Ohio Land Company, etc., etc."

My first encounter with Latin gave me one of the most unhappy fortnights of my youth. I entered Central High School in Omaha a few weeks late, as usual, with the result that the rest of the class in elementary Latin were engaged in exercises entirely unintelligible to me. I stuck it out for a time, but the others seemed so assured while I was so mystified that I decided to try some tutoring. A frail old scholar from Creighton, a Catholic school and college—Mr. Kenney—came to our house and together we sailed into the endings of the first declension.

We had not been at it for more than a half-hour before I realized suddenly that each of the five different endings had a precise meaning of its own. All one needed was to learn the meanings of the five cases and the paltry terminology concerning them, and the first declension was there and ready, in working order. I tutored for a week, just to make sure of things, and I began to enjoy the subject immensely. Our high-school Latin teacher was a tiny birdlike woman, swarthy and with sparkling dark eyes, graying hair, Mrs. Bessie J. Snyder. It was impossible not to learn Latin and like it under her tutelage.

So much is made nowadays of education and the terrible plight of all who lack one that I can scarcely believe, as I look back on it, the easygoing attitude taken by my parents and myself toward my own. It may well be that the course I followed—or perhaps did not follow—was disappointing to them, but not even my most unexpected starts and stops ever brought from them the least hint of disapproval. I cannot recall that either my father or mother ever reproved me over any issue of importance, no matter how discouraging my decisions might have seemed to them; neither can I think of any want that I ever made known to them that was not amiably gratified. I was, for my part, a reasonably dutiful son, not given to asking for the impossible, and intensely fond of my parents, and out of this warm family relationship there grew, I suppose, another easygoing assumption that I would eventually enter and carry on my father's hardware business. I certainly grew up in that assumption, just as I always assumed that I would inevitably go to Williams College. Why not?

A year of Omaha High School was more than enough for me. Other than the wonderful Mrs. Snyder, the teachers I had were, I thought, a sour lot. Perhaps I was getting too old to go along with more women teachers, and we all agreed that I should enter some preparatory school in the East. I should mention at this point two threats, or mock threats, with which my parents greeted real misbehavior on my part as a small boy: one, a summertime remonstrance, was that they would have to send me to a summer camp for boys; the other, that I was leaving them no choice but to send me to a military school—Shattuck, Culver, or whatever. Both ideas seemed to me equally repugnant, as I am sure they did to my family.

The selection of a school for me was as offhand as anything of this sort could be. I had been reading the Owen Johnson stories about Lawrenceville in *The Saturday Evening Post*; it sounded like an entertaining place, and I believe some arrangements were made in the spring of 1913 for me to go there in the fall. But early in the summer my mother met a personable young man in Williamstown, Karl Wells, who proved to be a master in a small school established some sixteen years earlier, the Morristown School in Morristown, New Jersey. His case for the small school of a hundred or so boys was persuasive, and since I cared not at all which school I attended— so long as it was not a military school—my father deposited me at Morristown that September, after several splendid days with him at the Waldorf.

I knew no more about the real composition of a community like Morristown than I did Omaha. At the time it seemed to me excitingly elegant, and so it was in many ways, providing glimpses of a style of living I had not seen before anywhere: a five-gaited hack—single-footing it along the road in long strides at what looked to be about 25 mph, the rider a bony-faced exercise man, seeming to sit without motion on the small saddle; some young people in a chain-drive Simplex, a hugely rumbling car with a small "close-coupled" body by Hol-

59

brook, the bows of its top (snugly folded down) of varnished light wood; some elaborate estates, such as Mrs. H. McK. Twombley's at nearby Convent, and the fantastic hilltop house with its stables, garages, and eighteen-hole golf course from which Otto Kahn was proposing to crash the highly stratified society of this self-satisfied suburb; many interesting houses; and always the sense of nearness to the much greater attractions of New York.

The boys at the school were a mixture of all sorts. The place was so small that everyone knew everyone else and all about one another. Reticence was not possible, and we probed each other's lives and minds with inexorable candor. There were six forms and about fifteen boys to a form—bright, dull, amusing, lazy, dirty, or dandified. Some were there simply to relieve their parents from thinking about them; others were expected to come home weekends and bring friends with them. There were two or three from California and one from Texas.

The founders and proprietors of the school were a triumvirate of Harvard '88 graduates: Francis Call Woodman, headmaster; Arthur Pierce Butler, vice-headmaster; and Thomas Quincy Browne, treasurer. Their scheme of a school was, I believe, sound and would have been a great success, had they been drawing on families less precariously situated than the banker-broker types of the on-the-way-up commuters. As it all turned out, the Depression very nearly did the school in, and left it on a five-day-a-week basis, which necessarily restricted attendance to boys who could go home each weekend. In its earlier days it was a conventional, strict, tightly controlled boarding school with a sprinkling of day boys from Morristown. The staff was good, and the Latin and Greek teacher, James A. Reeves, was, along with Mrs. Snyder of Omaha, the best and most stimulating within my experience. Most remarkable, as I look back on it, was the school's success in enabling boys so sluggish and indifferent as to seem ineducable to pass the College Board examinations and enter the college of their choice. Reeves went on to a considerable career after leaving the school, notably as the tutoring genius of Manter Hall, in Cambridge, Massachusetts. I was charmed to meet him in 1930 in Cambridge, when he confided to me an extraordinary statistic: it was just before Harvard had set up a tutorial system of its own, but the fact was, he said, that of some 3,000–3,500 undergraduates at Harvard, with its endowment of nine figures, close to a third in the previous year had recourse to Manter Hall, where the endowment consisted of two or three people like Jimmy Reeves and a few blackboards and bits of chalk, in rented premises. On the publish-or-perish proposition, I doubt that Jimmy Reeves ever published anything. He was a crammer second to none, but I think he was in the much larger sense a great teacher. His Latin and Greek gave me an abiding liking for words and language and a comfortable sense of having something to tie to amid the vague and often muddled choices in English grammar. That, I suspect, is why I so admired Latin in any case: a truly precise language, few idioms, and a clean-cut rule for everything; learn the rules, follow them, and no trouble can befall you. I liked Greek less, insofar as it seemed to me less precise and therefore somewhat sloppier. I realize that this makes me sound like an altogether conventional sort of person who thinks everything ought to be done according to what the book says, and I am somewhat shocked to find that this is probably true.

Morristown School was full of penalties for tardiness and other small offenses, for which "marks" were meted out—five, ten, twenty, as the gravity of the case required. The marks, each calling for one walk around the school's cinder track, were read out after luncheon, when the entire school and staff gathered in the main study hall for dismissal, and one had to walk off his marks before engaging in sports for the afternoon. Every moment of our day was prescribed and supervised, and even study, after classes were dismissed for the day, had to be carried on in the schoolroom—from 5:00 to 6:00 in the afternoon and from 7:30 to 9:00, five days a week. Since no other reading matter was allowed, one might just as well study the textbooks and let it go at that.

The school was especially strict about what we wore. Going without a necktie would have been unthinkable; for dinner the requirement was a dark suit, white shirt, and starched collar, which really necessitated a complete change from daytime wear. We tried at times to save time on the shirt change by folding the button-down collar inside the white shirt most of us wore by day, and buttoning over it a stiff collar that had been carried in a pocket. But this process left the buttons of the vanished button-down collar exposed, and the scrutineer master at the dining-room door would send back to change any boy disclosed to be wearing a "double-decker." Some boys went so far as to cut off the telltale buttons, but one really saved needless quarreling with the authorities for more substantial purposes. I am reminded of these exactions when I contemplate the school and college dress of today, not so greatly unlike the beatniks'. Granting that a dirty sweater, dirty slacks, and dirty shoes are inexpensive, convenient, and perhaps even comfortable for a young person who asserts he is not in the least interested in them anyhow, and whose ideas might be more significant than his appearance leads one to expect—granting all this, I am bound to wonder what becomes of these same people in later life, once the priceless insouciance of youth is gone. What is as embarrassing as the aging Boy Wonder, the superannuated Peter Pan, or the beatnik at fifty?

I went to Morristown for three years. At some point in my second year one of our better athletes, a boy named James T. Swan from Passaic, mentioned to me a scheme that had been flowering in his mind for some time. I liked him immensely for his maturity and his ready sense of mirth, and the scheme was a dazzler. It was no more than a matter of simple reasoning, beginning with the fact that there were several new boys in the school so dull and awkward and generally unprepossessing that, it seemed plain to us, they must have been a source of great worry to their parents. There must have been previous school experience for these boys that failed to pay off, and this, we felt, might have given the parents certain doubts, even distrust, of what school authority in general might report and recommend about their son. Would not these parents be glad to subscribe to a more intimate and disinterested report on the boy, not from the headmaster but from schoolmates in more direct day-to-day touch with the problem? Sports? Social relationships? Studies? Personality? For a weekly report for the rest of the school year the fee would be $100.

We picked the three richest and least promising of the new boys and drew up identical letters for their parents, laying out our own qualifications in no modest terms. We were staggered to receive by what must have been return mail in each case a check for $100: great idea, much interest, would look forward, and so forth. We turned to and began scrutinizing our subjects. All school grades were posted each week, and these were easily summarized, and I am sure it was no surprise to the parents that the grades were dismally low. Sports were of course seasonal, but these afforded us a paragraph or two on physical coordination, sportsmanship, and such. Since all sports were more or less compulsory, it was impossible not to have subject matter in this category for the taking.

Our reports went along breezily for a month or more. We even talked with the three boys and asked them idle questions. But what was soon troublesome was the fact that we were making the reports too conscientiously: it was becoming a frightful grind, especially since none of the boys showed any sign of improvement. How often could we repeat that "J——— spent the week practicing with the substitutes of the Third

Team. . .''? Or, "J—— seems still reluctant to engage in the give-and-take of informal discussions with the other boys in Form II''?

We decided by the end of about six weeks to call it off and, with some assistance from home, to refund the subscription fees in full, which we did with postal money orders. I know there was no collusion at any stage of this episode, for we kept it a dark secret, but all three of the parents—again by return mail—sent back the money orders, endorsed to us, and said, with only nominal variations of expression, that they had received their money's worth.

Swan and I felt we were well out of it all, but on becoming a bit pressed in the following year we tried it again. This time the very first parent we approached took it for what it might well have looked to be—a form of extortion—and complained to the headmaster. The latter was ready to talk expulsion and to regard our offense as monstrous, but our account of the previous year's satisfied parents—of whom he had not heard— and our incontrovertible statement that we felt sorry for the boy and thought he needed help took a good deal of the starch out of his moralizing. The matter was dropped on our agreement to sin no more.

The school was a curious set of cross-currents: a genuine, casual democracy and frankness among the boys, backed by preachments to that effect from the staff, and an inevitable tinge of sycophancy and lip-smacking in any mention by the authorities of the great or near-great among parents or boys, past or present, who had any connection with the school. We were allowed to draw 50 cents a week from the school bank as spending money, and we were formally instructed that money was far down the list of priorities toward which we should be striving. It was indeed the period of ostentatious wealth, and to spend a weekend at the home of one or another of our plutocrats was to sample a world of sumptuous novelty. There was one boy who lived not far from the school who was picked up each Saturday by a chauffeur in a vast Alco six-cylinder touring car, a model distinctive for the white band edging the top of its body-sides, and a very good car of the time. I went home with him one Saturday, and after luncheon —served by a butler and two footmen, the latter in brown tailcoats with silver buttons—his mother handed him money and told us that we could go to the theater in New York and dine that night at their rooms in Carlton House at—unforgettable number—22 East 47th Street. Her brother-in-law's valet would provide tickets and accompany us to the theater: *Chin-Chin* with Montgomery and Stone.

The chauffeur drove us to Newark, where we took a train to Manhattan, and by midafternoon we were at Carlton House in a lovely apartment: a pink bedroom, a blue one, and a living room where we would have dinner later on from the Ritz kitchen. What to do meanwhile?

"I'd like to go through the Tombs," said my host. "My father knows the District Attorney and I'll call up and see what he can do for us." The Ritz switchboard put the call through in no time, and whoever came on at the other end must have assented most hospitably, for my host, whom I will call G——, said we should be off immediately. It seemed to me an excellent way to spend the rest of the afternoon.

G—— asked the doorman to signal a cab for us and to pay the cab for taking us to the Tombs and to tip the driver and charge it all to the family's account. His mother had given him $50, he said, but there was certainly no use in spending his money on what could just as well be charged.

We walked up the steps of the grim old graystone building a few minutes later. A handful of men and women stood just outside the heavily barred doorway, apparently being denied admission. I was astonished, but G—— took it as no less than our due when a guard inside, very much on the lookout for us, asked our names and opened the barred door with a flourish. He would show us the whole place, he said, and answer any questions.

I remember the Tombs mainly for the servility of the guard toward G—— and myself and his rudeness to the prisoners, whom he identified for us well within their hearing: "Now this one here's an ordinary thief," as we stood at the barred cell door. "Here's a *murderer*, this nigger," he explained at the next. "We keep him by himself or with another nigger. We never put a white man in with a nigger." The prisoners, without exception, ignored the guard and ourselves, even though they might have wondered what business of ours their troubles could be. I recall a great stack of loaves of bread, the dirty appearance of the whole place, and its smelly airlessness.

G—— gave the guard grandly $1 when he unlocked the big door for us to leave. The doorman at Carlton House once again paid off the taxi on our return. For dinner that night I ordered my customary spree dish, spaghetti with tomato sauce, and a Clover Club cocktail, which impressed even my host, man about town though he was. It was delicious, the first I had ever tasted. I did not disabuse G—— of his impression that I rarely sat down to dinner without one.

Chin-Chin, which I saw a half-dozen times again during its long run at the Globe, was a rosy dream full of gay little chorus numbers, bright comedy, and a couple of songs whose words and music are still indelibly in my mind, "Ragtime Temple Bells" and "Chinese Honeymoon," this last a comic duet for the two principals. G——'s uncle's valet proved to be a Frenchman named Levasseur who sat in the balcony while we had orchestra seats, accompanying us after the show to the Hudson Tubes at 33rd Street and putting us on the train at Hoboken. Everything at G——'s house was quiet when we got there in the small hours, on foot, from the Lackawanna station. We were driven back to school that afternoon after another elaborately presented luncheon, this time with G——'s parents and two or three guests, who paid no attention to either of us.

As I look back at how we felt about the eight or ten real plutocrats in the school, I believe most of the boys had a sense of curiosity about where and how their families lived, but no great yearning to do likewise. It was like going to the theater to see one of these households in full swing, yet the human ingredient was not to be disregarded and that, after all, was what made the difference between great fun and little or none. The one material outlay that we all genuinely envied was the succession of stunning automobiles in which the little Kahn boy, in Form I, was delivered and picked up at the school each day: various Rolls-Royces, one a sports touring car with an aluminum hood and a thick panel of glass built into the body between the hood and the windshield; a Lancia or two; and a small imported car with much brass trim, either a Renault or a Fiat with the inverted-U radiator style, I forget which and it could just as well have been both. The Kahn chauffeurs were all foreigners, and in the winter they wore fur hats that matched the fur collars and cuffs of their livery greatcoats.

New York around the beginning of World War I had a glamorous quality that hardly seems credible to me today. It was a great run for one's money, and walking up Fifth Avenue in the 30's and 40's was always an adventure in new sights and sounds. I was waiting one day to cross Fifth Avenue at 34th Street when I saw the traffic policeman stopping all the cross-town traffic and clearing the intersection, beckoning on, meanwhile, whatever was coming down the Avenue. It proved to be a coach-and-four jingling past at a very fast trot, driven by a woman. She gave a nod to the policeman, who saluted her as the rig flashed by. Beside her on the box was an elderly man, and a liveried guard at the rear was blowing various calls on

67

a long coaching horn. A Dalmatian loped along between the back wheels.

As I crossed, I accosted the policeman. "Who was that?" I asked. "That, sir," he replied, with a genial smile, "was Inez Milholland Boissevain, out taking the air."

The shops, too, were like nothing I had known. Sulka was then, I believe, at 34 West 34th, a few doors from the Waldorf, renowned for heavy silk socks with all sorts of elaborations of clocking and design. Its neckties were fascinating but somehow a shade too frenchified for my taste, and there was really nothing that I needed or wanted that was not to be found in Brooks Brothers' store at 22nd and Broadway. Brooks offered many articles at that time which were simply not obtainable elsewhere. The prices were proper, and I have often wondered why their competitors were so slow in tapping the same sources of supply overseas that gave Brooks so wide a reputation. The 22nd Street store was still laid out on the old-style theory that only a few examples of the inventory should be displayed—and these in immaculate, cleverly lighted mahogany showcases —while all else was kept in noncommittal drawers and cupboards. I believe this theory was based on the belief that most of the Brooks customers knew what they wanted anyhow, and that the seemingly understated display technique gave an extra fillip to whatever was shown, which in my case was certainly the fact. I once bought a pair of high shoes, brown calf, brogued, that laced all the way up and were a great nuisance, simply because they looked so distinctive in a Brooks showcase and because I had never seen such a shoe anywhere else.

Private houses still survived along Fifth Avenue—brownstones, Greek temple motifs, imitation French châteaux, severely formal one-of-a-kind houses of no particular period but very handsome and well kept—all these piqued the stranger's interest, as did the smart carriages and exotic automobiles waiting outside at times, often with a footman as well as the chauffeur. The life inside these houses was pretty thoroughly blanked off from the passers-by, but there was one house on the east side of the Avenue in the upper 40's, owned, so we heard vaguely, by one of the Goulds, where just beyond the marble vestibule, through a second door of glass and decorative wrought iron, one caught a glimpse of the footman, a bewigged and powdered lackey in knee breeches and white stockings. He was the only one I have ever seen in real life on the job, and I found myself wanting to know more about him: whether he felt like a fool in such a get-up and whether he was paid extra for wearing it.

The motor traffic abounded in unique cars combining the latest and finest in engineering with the work of the great body-builders. A "custom" body was just that: made to suit the idiosyncrasies of a single owner and no one else and like no other in the world. It was not easy to identify the body-builder without inquiry, but some of them affixed a small nameplate to an inconspicuous part of the chassis. Brewster, the former carriage-maker, was probably the best known of the Americans, but there were many others—Judkins, LeBaron, Derby—and one could usually spot a Holbrook body by the narrow molding which this craftsman liked to put horizontally along the side of a touring-car body, some three inches below the top of the doors. Striping and panels of cane were continued from the days of carriages; sometimes even the whole back part of a "town car"—a closed car with no overhead weather protection for the driver—was varnished cane over a black shell. The striping was handwork of great delicacy, and hairlines, in red on navy blue, or yellow on black, to match a general color scheme, were much admired. Most of the great makes—Minerva, DeLaunay-Belleville, Isotta-Fraschini, Hispano-Suiza—from England and Europe have vanished altogether, and I can think of no American make of today that

69

was anything like a status symbol in those days. (One finds some dashing examples of elegant coachwork in the Museum of Carriages in Lisbon, one a small closed carriage of about 1840 in olive green with an almost imperceptible vertical orange stripe at about one-inch intervals and doorsills of intricately carved, polished tortoise shell.)

The best restaurants in New York, Sherry's and Delmonico's, occupied diagonally opposite corners at 44th and Fifth. I was not yet attuned to them and their muted connoisseurship, but I was impressed by the excellence of their food and service. For a schoolboy the greatest treat was to be taken to one of the big cabarets, such as Shanley's or Churchill's all but next door to each other on Broadway, or to Rector's just across the street. These places not only offered a first-class floor show at dinnertime and after the theater, but they actually competed energetically with each other as restaurants, and people went to them in expectation of a good meal and good service and got it, along with music and entertainment; $5 would provide generously for an outing for two at any of these places. I recall none of the cabaret entertainers as being at all celebrated, save for those at the Midnight Frolic on the New Amsterdam Theater roof, where stars of the Ziegfeld Follies often appeared, and I do not believe that huge salaries and "name" acts were at all the order of the day in most of the cabarets. The variety of choice was tremendous, for many of the hotels offered dinner and supper shows, and one could also try Murray's, Healey's, Reisenweber's, Bustanoby's—all quite good and with reasonable prices. I can think of no one of these places that ever seemed to deserve the word "gyp," or where I ever experienced the least unpleasantness. I find it hard to dine out in New York today without having to report exactly the opposite.

My mother and sister spent part of a winter in New York while I was in Morristown. My sister was studying under Her-

70

bert Fryer, an English pianist, and there were several evenings when we bought standing room at the Metropolitan, a manner of opera-going which estranged me permanently from Wagner but which, by great luck, brought us to the performance of *Carmen* in which Geraldine Farrar very nearly ended then and there the career of Enrico Caruso. They had been getting on each other's nerves, it transpired, and I must say that I could think of no more improbable figure for a romantic soldier-lover than this rotund little Italian, straining the seams of his white breeches, trying to balance his tin helmet nonchalantly on his knee and stay disentangled at the same time from a sword almost as tall as himself. The crisis came when Farrar, a big, strong girl in any company, was to repulse the advances of her quondam lover, which she did so enthusiastically as to fling him halfway across the Met's broad stage. Caruso was enough of a trouper to continue in the ring with her, but the story made all the papers the next day, and we felt we had witnessed something very special indeed.

I still count the little preamble that begins as the houselights go down and the footlights glow and goes on to accompany the slow rise of the curtain on the opening scene of *Carmen* as the most cunningly contrived passage of descriptive music I have ever heard. By the time the curtain is up and the big chorus makes itself heard, I am always willing to believe every note and syllable that follow. I believe the Metropolitan always hired an army of "supes" for its mob scenes and parades, and I was touched by the scanty number of bullfighters and their women who were available in a performance at L'Opéra Comique in Paris for the parade outside the bullring. These people were obliged to exit into the "arena" and then to run at top speed backstage and re-enter as part of the gay procession, while the spectators on the stage discovered and hailed them anew each time they came around. A parade can be made to

71

last indefinitely by this method, and the performers seemed to take extra pleasure in an ever so slight exaggeration of the incidental business in this circumstance. It is something of a feat to remain the arrogant *torero,* coolly accepting the plaudits of the multitude and trying meantime to get back one's wind.

●●

CHAPTER FIVE

Solo in Wyoming

I CAME OUT well enough in the College Board examinations, but I was short a credit in geometry and in the fall of 1916, I entered Williams in the class of 1920 with a "condition" in that subject. I still do not know what I expected college to be or what I would derive from it, beyond an interval of good company before eventually going to work. There was no specific objective of learning or achievement in my mind, and the idea that a college degree was in any way a credential that might be of use to me never entered my head.

A half-dozen of my new classmates quickly proved very pleasant company, and our major concern was how we would fare when, after a period of formal "rushing" by the fraternities, which took in the great majority of undergraduates, the final invitations went out to the freshman class in November. There was no one house where I felt at all certain of an acceptance, and I persisted in a vaguely reassuring expectation that something suitable would turn up. But as the weeks of rushing began and I was dined and scrutinized at one house after another, at no time did it seem to me that I was really getting anywhere with any of them. Hoping, nevertheless, right to the bitter end—an empty mailbox while those of my friends were stuffed with bids—I found myself totally rejected and this in a community completely dominated by the fraternity system. I would not even be seeing my friends at meals, for only the non-fraternity men ate at the Commons.

My haste was such that I did not even trouble to resign. I packed a bag, left a note asking my cousin to pack my trunk and ship it to me by express, and took The Century at Albany that evening, homeward-bound. For the first time in my life I had tested my standing with my fellows and been found ruinously wanting, and that was that. It simply could not be explained away or made more palatable: I was a flop.

So ignominious and speedy a withdrawal from college must have surprised and disappointed my parents, but never a hint of any such reaction came from either of them. I went to work at the hardware store, my father brightened my life considerably by trading in our old 1913 Chalmers "36" on the marvelous new Stutz, and I plugged along until the next summer, when we drove East once again. That fall I decided to have a try at the University of Chicago, where I was admitted as a student taking correspondence courses while tutoring and working off my condition in geometry, but living in an undergraduate dormitory, Hitchcock Hall. I even became pledged to a fraternity, and all was going along smoothly enough until I brought home two or three friends for a long Washington's Birthday weekend. At this point I was overwhelmed by one of the viral infections which smote me two or three times in my younger days, and I was seriously ill for a month. Again I withdrew from college.

It happened that James Morton & Son Company was supplying the hardware for a ranchhouse that an Omaha contractor was building on a vast property at Pitchfork, Wyoming, amounting to some 240,000 acres and shipping several trainloads of Herefords to market each year. It appeared that I could have a small job there as a tractor driver, for some 4,000 acres of the bottom land along the valley of the Graybull River were under cultivation, and I decided to take it on. It was the first for me of what were to be several adventures in Wyoming, a region that has never ceased to fascinate me. I can no longer tolerate the high altitudes of the Rockies, and I am long out of touch with developments there, but the ranch hands and small landowners of those days were certainly the most formidable and the most entertaining people I have ever met. I believe almost any one of them, given a rifle and an ax, could have fashioned a way of life for himself and lived off the country indefinitely.

To reach Pitchfork one took at Billings the branch-line train to the end of the railroad at Cody, and went from there by a light horse-drawn stage to Meeteetse, a little cow town some forty miles to the southeast, with a brick hotel—I believe it was the only brick-surfaced building for many miles around— the Weller House, where two and three guests to a room was the practice; a barber shop where a wood-burning stove heated water for the only bathtub in town available to the public (BATH: 50¢); a Chinese short-order restaurant which was the only really bad Chinese restaurant I have ever encountered; a large general store; a couple of saloons; and a livery stable. One of the saloons, operated by two brothers, Bob and Jack Fenton, was great fun, and I spent many of the final days of my stay in Wyoming playing solo there, from 9:30 in the morning to closing time toward midnight. Rickety board sidewalks and a few cow ponies sleeping at the hitching rails completed the Meeteetse scene.

Pitchfork was some twenty-five miles or more beyond Meeteetse, reached by what was called the Sunshine Stage, a light two-horse wagon which also carried the mail, fortunately for the passenger, for an excellent lunch was provided for the driver, by his contract with the Post Office Department, at a small ranch en route, and the passenger fared equally well at a cost of 50 cents. The Pitchfork brand, a design of three short prongs with a stubby handle, was famous all over the West, but Pitchfork itself, although shown on some maps, was no more than a ranchhouse and postal address, with a large barn and vast corrals of peeled logs. Nearby neighbors—in the Wyoming sense—were the Antlers Ranch at Sunshine and the Palette Ranch, one or the other of which was owned by the New York sportsman W. R. Coe. The brand of the Palette was an artist's palette.

Four ranches made up the Pitchfork complex: The Pitchfork, the Z–Bar–T, nine miles up the river from Pitchfork, another cattle outfit where the new house was going up and where I would be working; the 91, a horse ranch that was said to be doing a brisk business with the Army; and the TL, a sheep ranch that I never did get around to seeing. The scene as a whole was the broad, gently rolling brown bottom lands of the Graybull Valley, surrounded by rough and lofty snow-covered mountains. A pattern of haystacks, each protected by barbed wire, dotted the valley, and the main work of the cowboys from day to day was forking out hay to the Herefords, which were broken up into small groups and divided among many stacks, when the snow cover was too heavy for grazing. The weather was always spectacular, but even in early April the sun in the high altitudes was hot enough to keep the range fairly open, although the occasional blizzard might look like the end of the world. A dozen or more hands worked on the Z–T, some married and living with their families and others living in the bunkhouse, a rather too small room with six or seven beds and bunks, adjoining a dining room and kitchen.

There was no plumbing of any sort in the bunkhouse, but I believe the kitchen held a hot-water tank heated from a spacious coal or wood range. Soft coal was abundant and mined almost locally in that part of Wyoming. The washing water for the ranch hands was no more than a large bucket on top of the potbellied stove, with a dipper and a tin basin, and one emptied the basin out the door after using it. Just outside the bunkhouse an icy little brook called Rose Creek tumbled down the hill, and one could get fresh water from a pump outside. I preferred the pump to the tin basin, but it was a fast turn on a chilly morning. The outdoor privy for the hands was a commodious multi-passenger unit in a shed off the barn. The house at the Pitchfork ranch was adobe or plaster and rather picturesque, but the Z–T bunkhouse was nondescript—a one-story clapboard building.

I set up in the bunkhouse the folding canvas cot that I had brought along, but a couple of nights there were enough. It was customary for the last man to turn in to cram the large potbellied stove that heated the place with all the wood it could hold and then to make sure that the windows and door were tightly closed. A half-hour later the stove was cherry red, the room temperature impossibly high, and the whole place echoing with thunderous snores. I shifted to a small wall tent of my own on a gentle slope outside, where I managed to keep dry and fairly warm in a tight lamb's-wool sleeping bag and many layers of blankets.

The Z–T used various tractors, including a huge J. I. Case steamer, but I found myself on one of two small Cleveland caterpillars, of early design, in a tandem hitch pulling eighteen-foot double-disks, harrows, drills, and a manure spreader of discouraging voraciousness. It was shocking, after an hour of prying and heaving at the layers of the manure stack in loading the spreader, to find the whole cargo kicked off over the stern in what seemed hardly more than seconds. The old ranch hand in charge of our rig with whom I was working was named Wagner. Old Wag could outfork me by an embarrassing margin, and he could swear more impressively, as he did at the frequent breakdowns of our caterpillars, than anyone else on the place—longer, harder, and with more real conviction, so menacingly that one almost expected the misbegotten machine to heal itself and resume pulling. We used the caterpillars for all sorts of tasks, and my first job with them was as part of the tandem hitch when we went to work on a long, low log barn that was sagging heavily from one end toward the other. We hitched on to the ridgepole and pulled the structure into plumb, at which point log props were applied to the other end to keep it that way, and I don't believe this whole job took more than a half-hour.

One of the caterpillars was powered by a Buda engine, and this would quickly overheat and boil away its water every two or three circuits of the field. The other had a Wideley engine (although my spelling may not quite suffice), a much better power plant, but both tractors suffered from a ghastly need of frequent greasing, and both were prone to rupture their tracks and necessitate the most arduous repairs, on the spot and then and there. A lack of grease would cause the small idler wheels inside the track to freeze, which one discovered only after the track had ground away part of the wheel and produced a useless "flat" wheel. The other failing lay in the tendency of the heavy pins which connected the joints of track to work their way out and foul some part of the chassis. To make any repairs to the wheels it was necessary to dig a sizable hole, take out a pin from the track, and lower the ends of the track into the hole, thus getting direct access to the wheel. The ranch maintained a machine shop and plenty of spare parts for all the machinery, and a blacksmith whom I came to know very well, a tall, wiry Texan with faded blue eyes and thick, straw-colored hair and mustache, by the name of James Jefferson Knight. Along with the cook, an ex-Army mess sergeant in the Philippine war and the finest cook imaginable for such a crew as the ravenous hands of the Z–T, he was perhaps the toughest man on the place—sunny and amiable on the job but a rapid and morose souse once inside a Meeteetse saloon.

The incessant repairs and lugging water from the river with Old Wag in a ten-gallon milk can made a day's work with the tractors fairly heavy going. The cultivated acreage was four or five miles up the river from the bunkhouse, and our transport was a Model T, with the back seat removed and a platform at the rear where our gasoline and miscellaneous gear were carried. The route was cross-country, without any road, and almost any morning on the way up to our rig we would start up an antelope from the river; it would come flying up the slope, across our bows at perhaps 200 yards distance, and vanish over the hill in a matter of seconds, certainly the fastest animal at full throttle I have ever seen and seeming almost not to need to touch the ground.

When unencumbered by a tow, a small caterpillar was a furiously rough ride, veering and yawing at the slightest inattention on the part of the driver, for a touch on the steering wheel would brake it sharply on one track while leaving the other free, and in either hard-over position the machine could turn in its own length. Pulling a big load, it was much more stable, but as the driver of the rear tractor in the tandem I lived in a cloud of dust almost regardless of where the wind was coming from, getting the full output from the tractor ahead or from the machinery we were pulling behind. The massive white cloud formations, forever changing against the background of the blindingly blue mountain sky, were always worth watching as we roared along at a slow walking pace, with the unmuffled exhaust blasting away only a few feet from the driver's ear. Every so often a shadow would cross our course and looking up I could see an eagle, cruising the valley. I saw no other game on the Z–T, although the mountains were full of it. The Graybull was fished not at all except by the blacksmith, who would cut himself a willow rod, turn up a few "devil scratchers" from under the rocks along the bottom, and bring in a fine string of big trout after an hour or two of effort.

79

The high point of the day, socially, came for me after supper of an evening, when one of the foursome of solo players into which I had been admitted would look us over and remark, with an air of jovial inspiration, "Deal the cards, you sons of bitches, and I'll frog without looking." This was, in bunkhouse parlance, the Invitation to the Waltz, a frog being the lowest bid in solo and not really a very hazardous offer. But it always got a game going in the bunkhouse and we played there almost every night.

Solo is such a fast up-and-down sort of game that it is not easy to fix a satisfactory stake for it, especially if the players are hard up, as we were. Unless one gives the chips a precise money definition, the pastime version of solo is to start each of the four players with 110 chips, and the first to go broke pays a flat sum to the other three. A solo hand can be played very quickly indeed, and if one considers that the bidder of heart solo—the highest bid—could win as much as $18 on a single hand at 5 cents a point, played out in a minute or less, even a penny game can reach interesting dimensions. The ordinary all-day saloon game was on the basis that the first to lose his stack of 110 chips would buy a round of drinks for the others. There were really no saloon bums in Meeteetse, and it was good manners to include the kibitzers, when the players stepped up to the bar, for they were kibitzers only because they lacked numbers to make up a game of their own, and they would treat in their turn like everyone else. A great virtue of solo is that it can be played by either three or four players without any change in its values, since in the four-handed game the dealer lays off. I believe it stems from the German game called skat. I have never found it in the East, but the plain fact is that any game favored by such gamblers as the stock-hands of Wyoming is worth a try. I marvel, looking back, at how hard they worked for their small wages and how gaily they risked their all. My own ratings would be, approximately:

the best game for two, pinochle; for three or four, solo; for four, hearts; for five or six, straight draw poker or five-card stud.

Solo is easier to play than to explicate, but for anyone interested in cards, here is the game:

A hand of solo is played by three players; if there are four, the dealer lays off after dealing. It is a bidding game in which the declarer becomes opposed by the other two playing as partners. The objective of the declarer is to gain "count" rather than to win tricks, the count being the same as in pinochle (ace—11, ten-spot—10, K—4, Q—3, J—2, for a total of 120). The declarer is paid by each of his two opponents for any count above the break-even point of 60, and he pays each of his two opponents the amount by which he fails to take in 60. As in pinochle, the ten-spot is next to the ace in value in the play as well as in the count.

Solo is played with the six-spot low, the two's, three's, four's and five's being removed at the beginning of play. The first round of the deal is three cards at a time to each of the three players and a "widow" or "kitty" of three face-down in the center of the table. Four at a time to each of the three players are dealt in two more rounds, and the dealer's duties are completed, leaving each player with eleven cards in hand and three, face-down (of course the entire deal is face-down), in the center of the table.

There are only three bids in solo: a frog, the lowest, in which hearts are automatically trumps and the bidder, if he becomes the declarer, is allowed to take the widow into his hand and put face-down in front of him, before play begins, any three cards from the total of fourteen that he is holding and these belong in his eventual count; a solo, in which clubs, diamonds, or spades may be the trump, according to the declarer's later announcement, and which overcalls a frog; and a heart solo, which makes hearts trumps and overcalls all other bids and which, if bid initially, ends the bidding then and there. In all solos, including a heart solo, the widow becomes the property of the declarer but remains face-down on the table, undisclosed, throughout the play. Any count it contains belongs to the declarer, but it cannot be turned over until the hand is played out.

The payoff rates on the three bids are: on a frog, one for one; on a solo, two for one; on a heart solo, three for one.

Examples, if the declarer happens to take in a total count of 72 for instance: on a frog he would win 12 points from each of the two opponents; on a solo 24 points from each; on a heart solo, 36 points.

Similarly, if he happened to fail to make 60 and took in, for instance, only 45, he would pay each of the two opponents 15 points on a frog, a solo, and a heart solo. All suits have the same value, so that the first player to bid a solo can be over-called only by a player bidding a heart solo. The trump which the player has selected for his solo in clubs, diamonds, or spades is not identified until the bidding is complete, at which point a player will remark to the declarer, "You bid a solo. Put a handle to it," and the declarer announces the trump.

There are very few rules indeed governing the play. The opening bid is from the player to the left of the dealer, and the opening lead is from the player to the left of the declarer. A player must follow suit and if unable to do so must play a trump, regardless of how the trick stands at that point.

The Fenton brothers, a highly picturesque pair, were genial hosts to the two or three solo tables that were more or less constantly in use when we were in Meeteetse on an outing. The older Fenton was dressed as no one else in the vicinity was dressed, a cloth cap and a cardigan sweater setting him apart from all others. His brother had a long, ragged mustache, wore a shapeless and battered old felt hat, a vest and never a coat, and kept a much-used towel tucked into his waistband. He was extremely polite to me, and whenever he served me a drink he would whip out the dirty towel and polish the glasses with it before setting them down on the bar. (A drink was two ounces of Yellowstone whisky accompanied by a small beer chaser.) Both Fentons wore neckband shirts, with a brass collar button and no collar. The biggest night at their place, or for that matter in Meeteetse while I was there, was when Dr. Dorrance, the multi-millionaire owner of Campbell's Soup Company, was passing through with a large pack outfit on a spring bear hunt and decreed that everything for everybody at both saloons for the afternoon and evening would be on him, a *gala* which must still keep his memory green.

Getting the twenty-five miles to Meeteetse from the Z–T was a problem. Anyone with a truck or a car would offer a ride, but there were long periods, often several days at a time, when no one at all went over the tortuous road through the sagebrush and the countless prairie-dog villages. The only dependable method was to start walking and hope for a lift, but I walked it several times with never a sight of a ride. By about the halfway point the chattering and scurrying of the prairie dogs became a great irritant. The legend was that they could duck into their burrows too quickly even for a rifle shot, although I doubt this, but I never saw a dead one. They were not scavengers, but I was assured that no one but an "Injun" would eat one.

The blacksmith was usually my companion on a Meeteetse outing. Aside from his extraordinary skill at his forge, I remember him for his brown-paper Bull Durham cigarettes, which he twisted into a durable shape without licking the paper, and for his boast that he could tell time by consulting a two-foot carpenter's rule that he carried. I had many a chance to check him on this last, and I have no way of explaining his success. He would unfold the rule and bring down his thumb at some random point on it, meditate a moment, and then

83

announce, within ten or fifteen minutes of exactness, the time of day. The figure where his thumb had come down had nothing that I could see to do with what he announced as the time. He was oddly mystical in his purported disclosure of his method, which went as follows and no further:

"Now there's twelve inches in a foot, ain't there?"

"Correct."

"And it's twelve hours around the clock?"

"Right."

"And there's twenty-four inches in two feet?"

"Right."

"And there's twenty-four hours in a day?"

"Yes."

"Well, there you are!"

The blacksmith's brown-paper cigarettes remind me that no one in Wyoming smoked "tailor-mades," which were regarded with suspicion no matter what brand and were usually called "pimp-sticks." Bull Durham was the universal smoke, with Duke's Mixture a poor second. I was the object of some curiosity by an old stockman in the Fentons' one day when I produced a package of pimp-sticks and lighted one. The old man looked at me with amazement and finally, unable to resist the opportunity, said to me, "Say—let me just try one of them things."

A few years later, on a long and enchanting motorcycle trip with my wife through France, we stopped at a pump outside a hotel in Châteaubriant. The porter was wearing a long apron of striped ticking and a visored cap and I took him for a Frenchman. But he noticed a Bull Durham tag hanging from my breast pocket and disclosed himself as an American from California. He had gone AWOL at the end of World War I and been stranded in his porter's job ever since. He asked me if I would give him the half-empty sack of Bull, but I dug into the locker and produced a couple of full sacks for him which had a profound emotional effect on him. "I save up for a ticket home," he said, "but just as I get almost enough to buy it, I blow it all on getting drunk. But I'm gonna start saving again right now." He looked over his shoulder and lowered his voice. "These frogs," he said, "are mean when you have to work for them."

The walk to Meeteetse was such a nuisance that I decided to buy a horse, and the foreman of the Pitchfork, a pleasant and much-respected man named Ott Casady, said he had just the right animal, an eight-year-old sorrel mare who had been running free on the range for the past year. The mare, I learned, would be brought in with a hundred or more other horses at the weekend, she would be mine for $40, and he would lend me a saddle and bridle while I tried her out. Her arrival at the corral of the Pitchfork one noon was part of a magnificent demonstration of professionalism by Casady and his men. Casady was the only man on the place who wore anything fancy in the way of chaps. His were gray leather, with a decorative motif in silver studs, emphasizing the three-pronged fork of the Pitchfork brand. I do not know where he got them, but the catalogues of the Miles City Saddle Company were the favorite reading matter in the bunkhouse of the Z–T, and one could find warrant in them for spending into the thousands on an equestrian outfit. Most of the style of the cowboys and hands was functional and without ornament. Casady, in his handsome chaps and riding a powerful big horse that carried his bulk like a feather, was an impressive sight.

A truck gave me a lift to Pitchfork. Casady and two or three of his hands were taking their ease on the top rail of the corral fence. Several branding irons were keeping hot in a small wood fire. There were many colts in the herd, he said, who had spent their first year without ever seeing a man, and he thought they would all be coming along any minute now.

85

He pointed across the flat where, two or three miles distant, one could see dust. "There they are," he said.

The dust, approaching at an amazing pace, disclosed a great mass of horses, running hard, guided and urged on by three or four riders, waving their hats and heading the whole thundering, breathless advance into the wide fan-shaped fencing that would funnel it into a lane leading to the corral. The horses were scarcely slowed by the lane, and the first arrivals burst into the big enclosure on the dead run, keeping at it in a counter-clockwise circling that was soon slowed by their sheer numbers. To me it was a scene of wild confusion, but Casady and his men could identify an astonishingly large number of the horses, some by name, others by their previous ownership or for some distinctive habit or accomplishment. They all identified the sorrel mare readily enough, and one of the hands, at what seemed to me the risk of his life, took his coiled rope and dropped down into the milling mass. His throw was so effortless that he seemed to move no more than his wrist, but his twitch on the rope brought the mare down, tripped by his noose on a foreleg, and he had a bridle on her in a jiffy. She was slick and very frisky, and I rode her back to the Z–T with much self-esteem. I unsaddled her in the barn, led her to a pasture, and turned her loose. This was a mistake. It was like stalking a wild animal on foot to get her into a corner and put a bridle on her the next time out.

I will not dwell on the trials I endured from this horse. She was mean and never mean the same way twice. She would tolerate two automobiles and bolt from the third, the same with mailboxes or even a stone beside the road. At times she would stop and eye a telephone pole with such trembling, ears-cocked, ears-back panic that even I began to think the pole was doing something to scare her; if not at that moment, perhaps it had on some previous occasion. At that instant, after seeming to compose herself, she would bolt again. She very nearly threw me when the sleeve of my slicker, neatly tied on behind me, came adrift and touched her flank to which her reaction was one of bucking and sunfishing. If I left her at a hitching rack, she would lean back and pull until she broke the reins. It was suicidal to light a cigarette while riding her in the dark. My worst moment with her came when we put up suddenly from the road just in front of us an eagle or a hawk which had been enjoying a dust bath. She went through her entire repertoire.

Casady obligingly took her off my hands. He decided that she was locoed, suffering from nervous instability caused by eating locoweed. In season, the weed produces an attractive little flower, and one of a cowboy's duties is to keep the stock from grazing on it, for it affects cattle as well as horses.

There were many odd characters at the Z–T: a Swiss chore-boy who lavished all his spare time and money on an ill-matched team and a buggy of which he was very proud, in the manner of a large property owner; an old Swede, Andy, perhaps eighty years old, who kept all his belongings—including a kerosene table lamp and china shade—in a tin trunk with a curved top and who could take a spading fork and prepare the ground for a huge kitchen garden in one long day of non-stop work; Doc, the self-styled veterinarian, forever fending off ribaldries about the mortality and strange symptoms his treatments were causing among the cattle; a cowboy known only as Big Red, soft-voiced, polite, and by far the biggest man in the whole countryside; a remarkably disheveled man named Brown, who lived with his two or three children in a sheep wagon, in which they would come in for supplies at long intervals from his job of keeping the barbed-wire fences in repair; John Sayles, the foreman, who could have stepped comfortably into a role in *High Noon* or *Shane,* who knew the scores of verses of "The Chisholm Trail" and many other marvelous ranch songs. The most amusing man in this assortment was a teamster whose name I have lost who arrived one spring evening as we were all sitting on the steps of the bunkhouse after supper. He was riding a large, dispirited horse and followed by a white pack mule carrying his bedroll and effects. He dismounted, opened the gate to the yard, and found himself defied by the mule, which balked and refused to be led or dragged or booted through the gate. No greetings had been exchanged, but finally a voice from the steps broke the silence.

"That's a fine big horse you've got there, friend," said the voice. "Whyn't you put a rope on the critter and haul him in?"

The stranger continued struggling with the mule, which relaxed suddenly and came ambling into the yard. "I would'a," the stranger called back to the group on the steps, "but the tree of that old saddle's a mite weak."

The next morning at breakfast, while the men were already tucking away their gargantuan portions of wheatcakes, potatoes, and ham and bacon from the ranch's smokehouse, the cook was standing in his kitchen doorway when the stranger appeared. "Hello," remarked the cook to no one in particular, "Here's the *mule man* again!"

Such a start could have blighted the affairs of some men, but the mule man was no novice at settling in and he was enough of a prima donna to take such a crack as almost a compliment, much as Henry Ford might have indulged those who joked about his Tin Lizzie. He was so full of talk and tall stories of his adventures that he quickly made himself at home. He was, incidentally, the only man I met in Wyoming who still wore a revolver at all times, a .38 double-action Smith & Wesson, from which most of the bluing had long been worn away, and he was fond of exhibiting an almost illegible permit to carry the gun issued in some small town in Montana many years earlier: a certificate, if you please, of his respectability and status in the community.

The mule man was a tireless solo player and the first, after supper each evening, to take the big plug-tobacco tin with the basket-like handles and sort out a deck from the mixture of greasy cards it contained. I do not remember that anyone ever put a new deck into circulation at the Z–T, and since such a player as the mule man smoked a cob pipe *and* chewed tobacco as he played, the cards all showed the effects of much fingering over months and years. His stories were bizarre; one was a description of a mysterious pestilence which littered the banks of some river in the Northwest with millions, said he, of dead salmon. "And sir," the story concluded, with the mule man assuming the air of one who could not expect such un-traveled folk as ourselves to believe him, "there warn't a dog nor a coy-o-tee for miles around as had a hair on his body for eatin' 'em!"

By far the most spectacular man on the Z–T was the cook, Red Carlin, a powerful-looking figure of middle height, a brick-red complexion, sparse ginger hair, bloodshot eyes, and a saturnine view of all authority. Like his small bedroom and the kitchen, his attire was always immaculate: a chef's white hat, a white shirt and trousers and several layers of aprons, and white sneakers as spotlessly clean as everything else he wore. He would replace immediately any garment that became the least bit stained. His pies were of absolutely classic delicacy, and I believe he would have been welcomed as a great cook any-where in the world. He was very kind to me and invited me into the kitchen for coffee and a bit a pie or cake whenever I was in the vicinity between meals, which was all too rarely.

Red disappeared for a day or two on drinking sprees in Meeteetse every few weeks, but he was too good a cook to be fired for such lapses. His ultimate departure came when he brought back to the ranch from one of these outings a stocky little chap who looked not unlike Red himself, an unemployed teamster whom he introduced to us as Shorty Towle. Alcohol was forbidden on the ranch, but Red and Shorty, as a nonworking guest, continued to hit it up in great style, and after a few days it was decreed by the proprietors that Shorty would have to go.

Red's response to this order, which came while he was turning a great outlay of steaks on his grill for our noon dinner, was to leave the whole meal to go up in smoke, telephone to Meeteetse for an automobile to pick him up, pack his suitcase, and, in his unfamiliar "store clothes" sit on the steps with Shorty awaiting their ride to town. His successor, who arrived a few days later, after an interval of what seemed to us semi-starvation, was hopelessly incompetent and as dirty as Red had been scrupulous. It was August, and I had been there almost five months. I decided to go home.

In Meeteetse I found that Red was lodged somewhere nearby and spending most of his time in the poker game, based in a log cabin at the edge of the village, a public-private sort of game where almost anyone was welcome to sit in. The game was straight draw poker or five-card stud, table stakes and everything in cash, and it worried me to find Red so heavily involved in it when I dropped in at the cabin one night. Pots of a couple of hundred dollars were commonplace. It was quite beyond my resources, and I was superstitious enough—and still am in gambling matters—to be worried too lest my presence somehow affect Red's luck adversely, for he seemed to be losing considerable money on fairly good cards. I slipped out without attracting his attention and decided to restrict myself to the small time solo game at the Fentons'.

The final week of my sojourn in Meeteetse brought me a casual meeting with Shorty Towle one day at the Fentons'. He had gone to work hauling coal and supplies to an oil-drilling rig some fifteen miles back into the hills, and he invited me to throw in with him in the sheep wagon in which he was camped on the bank of Wood River, a couple of miles south of town. It gave my whole stay in Wyoming a marvelously pleasant wind-up.

The routine was simple enough but Shorty's four-horse hitch —young, aggressive, and unpredictable animals that he called affectionately "my ponies"—made our daily travels exciting enough. At the end of each afternoon Shorty took on a ton or so of soft coal in his heavy freight wagon by pulling up under the hopper of a Meeteetse dealer, only two or three minutes and no work being needed for this process. He next picked up the day's supplies at the general store and a pint of whisky at the Fentons' for himself, and we were back at his camp by twilight. The horses were corraled at a bend in the stream, where they could drink at will, a vertical cliff forming about half of the enclosure and a crude fence of logs and wire the rest. They were fed hay and grain, and it was unsafe to get near the rear of any one of them, for they would kick eagerly at anything or nothing. Harnessing them of a morning was an exercise in delicate slow motion, as if we were handling unstable explosives.

Shorty's standard of housekeeping in the sheep wagon was as severe as Red's in his kitchen. Everything was scrubbed and in perfect order. He was a good cook and we lived very well, largely by his practice of helping himself to any part of the oil driller's supplies that he fancied. The drillers were highly paid, only the best of everything would suffice for them, and we prospered accordingly. Shorty's best specialty was a baking-powder bread which, cooked in a frying pan on top of the stove, came out as a single, light, skillet-sized biscuit. "Sheepman's loaf," Shorty said it was called, and it went very well with eggs and ham and bacon. The wagon contained an astonishing number of cupboards and drawers and a double bunk, crosswise, at its front end.

As a last act before putting out the lantern and turning in of an evening, Shorty put the pint of whisky to his lips and let the equivalent of three or four big drinks trickle down his gullet in the fashion of a Spaniard getting under a jet from a wineskin; he was the only man I ever saw who could take on whisky like that, without swallowing. In the morning, on getting out of his blankets and before firing up the stove, he tipped up the bottle again for most of what remained. The liquor seemed to affect him not at all, beyond bringing from him a sigh of satisfaction.

Our route to the oil derrick was altogether cross-country, with no roads at all but the faint track made here and there by the wagon itself on previous trips. The freight wagons had brakes of a sort, an iron shoe that could be made to press against the broad metal rims of the back wheels, activated by a cross-member terminating on one end in a socket into which a wooden pole was driven. From the upper end of the pole a stout rope went to the driver's seat, sometimes to a pedal, more often to a cleat, hanging loosely and ready for him to haul on by hand; the longer the pole, the greater the leverage and pressure on the brakes. Cross-country driving with a relatively light load like ours for four horses is easy enough on the level or uphill, but some of the dry gulches we crossed were so steep that much braking was needed to keep the wagon from over-running the horses. At one slope in particular it was all Shorty could do to hold them back from bolting. One of his "ponies" had dropped dead here some weeks earlier, he explained, and he had dragged the carcass down the gulch a few rods where its bones were already beginning to whiten. "They get a whiff of it along about here," he said, "and they don't like it a-tall."

The biggest freight wagon I saw in the West was the beer wagon, which came over the road from Cody to Meeteetse every month or so, a high-sided mountain wagon, piled to the sky with cases of beer from a Billings brewery; it had huge wheels, a lofty brake-pole, and a broad seat where the driver and one or two companions, beer bottles in hand, enjoyed the pleasures of a trip that must have taken at least two full days at a slow walking pace. One could imagine the wagon lurching and creaking over the stones of the river crossings, its ten or a dozen horses scrambling for a footing, and all Meeteetse turned out for its approach. With such an audience the driver became the stylist: it seemed almost without attention on his part, save for a ceremonial crack of the whip, that he turned the long hitch around and brought the wagon to a triumphant stop, the traces settling into the dust, at precisely the door of the Fentons' saloon.

I never learned how the drill came out, but a lot of wild-catting in the vicinity paid off in later years. The rig that Shorty was supplying was a study in loneliness, with no sign of other human existence to be seen in any direction. The drill and its steam engine were clanking and chuffing in all vigor when we got there, but it looked to me like a very long shot; the little pile of coal that we augmented so slightly seemed a trifling resource for powering so ambitious a venture. The silence when the drilling stopped for the dinner hour was overwhelming.

Dinner with the dozen or more drillers was superb. The men lived in a well-kept bunkhouse and took their meals in the cookhouse, presided over by a middle-aged woman and her beautiful daughter, perhaps twenty, and it was plain both were treated as the absolute authorities, having the unquestionable last word over everyone else on the premises. Their cooking alone could have warranted such a status; their dinners might have come from the kitchen of a rich Iowa farm at threshing time; but they were remarkable personalities into the bargain: warmhearted, gay, zealous, and amiably in complete control of their work and their environment. The hospitality of the whole establishment to such outsiders as Shorty and myself was a tonic to be felt all the way back to Meeteetse as our empty wagon rattled over the hummocks of buffalo grass. I can only hope that both women went on to marry wildcatters who struck it rich.

My worries about Red Carlin's poker-playing were needless, I found a year later, when I went through Cody with a friend from Indiana, at the beginning of a pack trip into the Shoshone Mountains. We dropped in at the Cody Café for breakfast, and there was Red, the proprietor, once again in his white aprons, giving me a comradely greeting. He had just about cleaned out the Meeteetse poker players, I learned, and he bought the café with part of his winnings.

Two years after that, in the second year of our marriage, my wife and I were in Cody on our way to the wilds. It was her first experience of Wyoming, and I was eager to have her see Red Carlin, whose saga I had told her, so we began the day, after stepping out of a stuffy Pullman into the chill of the early morning, at the Cody Café.

Red was not there. I asked the waitress about him. She was one of those types who seem always to have one hand at her hip and the other patting her back hair, and she looked at me superciliously. "Ain't you heard?" she asked.

"No, not at all. Heard what?"

"He ain't here any more. He's dead."

Her manner was so portentous that I could not help asking how it had happened. She seemed, also, to be disapproving of me already as a friend of Red's.

"He married one of the waitresses, and he killed her with a butcher knife," the waitress said. "And he hung himself in the jail at Fort Collins." I did not learn what had brought Red to Fort Collins, and I may be mistaken about the location, but that is what I thought the waitress said. At any rate, Red was dead by his own hand, and the customers of the Cody Café were the poorer for his passing.

●●●

CHAPTER SIX

Williams College: Final Venture

I WENT BACK to work in the hardware store after getting home again from Wyoming. I had tried to get into the Army's balloon school at Fort Omaha, but my myopia was so disqualifying that the examining doctor doubted whether even the Quartermaster Corps would have me. In a draft examination, I was able to memorize most of the eye-test chart before taking off my glasses. The doctor, seeing them in my hand, held them up and looked through the lenses. I should get a new prescription, he said, for my vision was too good for lenses of such power. But the war ended a month later, quite without my help.

College terms had been disrupted by the war, and most of them were to reopen in January, 1919, for what would be counted as a full academic year. I decided to give it all another whirl and see what might happen, and this time I thought I would try Harvard. I mailed my credentials to the dean of admissions and ate my Christmas dinner with a boyhood friend at Young's Hotel in Boston, a naval reserve ensign who had just returned from overseas. It was a wonderful dinner, coming in the last great days of a great dining room and it ended, unforgettably, with a Raspberry-Vanilla Mousse, a lavish conversion of cream, egg yolks, and fruit into a velvety richness. I was informed that my father, who had said nothing at all to me about it, had set up an account for me at the hotel and had deposited a handsome sum to my credit, against my college needs.

The day after Christmas I presented myself to the dean of admissions, who received me coldly. My credits, he said, devised for Williams, were short by a chemistry or physics credit for Harvard's purposes, and he would not entertain the idea of a condition in my case. I do not know whether he was speaking the whole truth, and I do not know who he was, but it was obvious that he was poorly impressed by me and my dossier. He gave me what I thought then and still think was wise advice. "I think," he said, "all things considered, that you should go back to Williams." Nothing could have been further from my plans up to that point, but I felt, suddenly, that he was quite right. I thanked him, gathered my documents, bowed out, went back to my hotel and drew out my credit in cash, and took an afternoon train to Williamstown.

I must say in behalf of the authorities at Williams that my abrupt reappearance and proposal to join the class of 1922 were accepted with great suavity and without even the lift of an eyebrow by anyone. Most of the friends I had known before were there and greeted me cordially when college reopened a week later. I shared a sunny suite in Williams Hall with a member of '21, and the winter bowled along uneventfully. I was even invited to join a fraternity, which I did eagerly. From this new circle I gained two delightful new friends, but I am afraid neither they nor I were of the stuff from which undying brotherhood is fashioned, if the commitment had to include the grotesquely bad cooking that was our portion at the fraternal board. We set up a table at the Williams Inn, where Lucius Treadway was making a beginning of his truly splendid career as a hotel magnate; we were joined by a pair of congenial non-students who were spending the winter at a local tutoring school; and the food and company resulting from these arrangements were quite the pleasantest part of my stay at Williams.

In sober after-thought, I think Williams was remarkably dull, its offer at the time no more in the academic sense than an extension of preparatory-school instruction. The faculty members whom I happened to draw were a humorless lot, reiterating the same routines year after year, and I can recall no personality of the staff whose laurels were anything other than those of seniority. I collected four B's and a D at the end of the college year, and it was irritating to get back a piece of translation or a composition without the touch of a correcting pencil on it and a bland B for a grade.

Even so, I might have drifted along in college for another year or two, but I was increasingly preoccupied with the hope of marrying the girl from the Seashore House, and her assent, toward the end of that summer, sealed my decision to begin trying to earn a living.

I am cheered to remember one wonderful achievement by Williams College, matched by few others and just as successful today, so I am told, as it was a half-century ago: the honor system. This was simply an assumption by all concerned that no student would cheat on an examination. It meant, in operation, that all examinations were unsupervised. A student came to the classroom at the scheduled time, picked up a blank book and a copy of the examination paper from stacks on the professor's unoccupied desk, and fell to work. He was free to come and go as he wished, perhaps to invite some friend in the class to go out for a cigarette; he could even take paper and book down to Gus Bridgeman's one-arm lunchroom on Spring Street and eat his breakfast, mulling it all over, if he had made a late start and missed breakfast. His only obligation was to turn in his paper at the end of the examination period.

Many contrasts with the Williams honor system turn up in the news from time to time. I think, especially, of the West Point episode and the flood of sympathy poured out by sports writers, Congressmen, educators, and commentators on the astonishingly large number of transgressors—fine, upstanding young Americans these, who never should have been made parties, willy-nilly, to an arrangement so unnatural, so foreign to the way most people feel about such things. The weeks of official bewilderment at the Air Force Academy when an identical problem became known raised the same doubts all over again: was it really necessary to take a bit of cheating so *seriously?* At Williams, it was good form to outwit the proctor at compulsory chapel—and there were hilarious ways of doing it—but that was a proctored situation with no quarter asked or given. From my own experience there I must report that I never saw or heard a hint of the least breach of the honor system by anyone.

I have never been able to find any really good reason why I was so inevitably destined to go into my father's hardware business. I do not believe there was ever a chance that I would progress in it, certainly not to any substantial degree, or that I should have been satisfied if I had gone ahead successfully and stayed with it. Some such realizations must have troubled both my father and my mother at the time, and I am fascinated, in retrospect, by our almost total failure to communicate usefully with each other on so immediate and important a problem. Our family relationship was one of love and trust; my parents were ready to make great sacrifices to help me get started in the world; yet the only course we could envision for me was that I should spend an indeterminate number of years "learning" the hardware business.

Older people in almost any sort of business must reassure themselves fairly steadily in the belief that their business takes a good deal of time to learn; for the businessman who is stupid or incompetent, it will take just that much longer, and there must be many who never do reach an understanding of their affairs. These last would be the most thoroughly convinced that business is a mysterious art, requiring a lifetime of experience on the job, before one can begin to make head or tail of it. Some of the stupidest men I have ever met told me, in all solemnity, that if I were to put in thirty years at plugging away as they had done, I might some day dream of holding down the bad job in which they were so permanently stalled.

So, it was not that the hardware business was so complicated or so hard to "learn," but rather a question of what to do about it after learning it. In my case the answer was: nothing. It was simply not in the cards that my father could ever bring himself to believe that I knew much—certainly not enough— about his business, or that between us we could find a way of working together fruitfully. Fortunately for me, I found this out fairly early, after, I should say, about four years of a more or less undemanding apprenticeship and two years of attempting to put some of my schemes and ideas into action. The relationship with my father remained perfect except for anything to do with James Morton & Son Company: the business was his domain, to run as he saw fit and with no time for answering the questions that I was forever asking him. I think he may have preferred to evade altogether the more serious questions that I raised, and there were many omens in the '20s that profound changes in distribution of hardware and everything else were in the making. Manufacturers were beginning to bypass their own dealers and jobbers and to sell directly to a sufficiently large customer. Chain-store competition, new display techniques, sales and promotion methods— all these demanded energetic reaction from even a small business like ours, but my father was actually too busy from day to day, too hard-driven by responsibilities of the moment, to take thought about what might or might not happen in years to come.

Why anyone would wish to establish a retail hardware business seems to me unaccountable. It calls for a heavy capital investment in a relatively slow-moving inventory; the cost of doing business is commensurate with that in many other kinds of retailing, but the profit margin is small and constantly being chipped away by competition; and there is scarcely ever an opportunity to make anything remotely like a killing—a large lump of profit by some shrewd or farsighted stratagem. The underlying reason for this state of affairs is that most of the items in a hardware store are bought and sold according to precise specifications: there is no way of persuading a customer to pay $5 for an item when the identical item, by name, number, and possibly size, is being sold for $4 by someone else. In a sense, a hardware store is like a bookshop, where the merchant must operate within the profit margin of either a fixed price, as in the case of books, or a price determined by competition which is likely to be even lower. The bookseller has a special advantage in being allowed to return for credit to the publisher any books remaining unsold six months after their delivery. The only dispensation of this sort in our business was the agency that my father held for years for Gifford-Wood Ice Tools, very expensive and specialized tools and machinery for harvesting natural ice in the days before mechanical refrigeration. The Gifford-Wood products were so good that they constituted very nearly a natural monopoly, with hardly another competitor, and they were held by us on consignment; we paid nothing for them, simply storing and selling them to users, and remitting the selling price to the manufacturer after deducting our commission.

I am reminded, in passing, of certain other items which had made an almost monopolistic place for themselves by sheer excellence and nothing else. A railroad brakeman or switchman, for instance, would buy only a switchman's lantern made by the T. L. Moore Company, in San Antonio, Texas; it was the only article made by Moore that we sold, and most of our other lanterns were made by a large company by the name of Dietz, but the railroad man, whose life and job often depended on his signaling lantern, wanted Moore's. A small company by the name of Buck Brothers made the only burnisher—a wooden-handled tool of polished steel used for smoothing the edge of a newly sharpened scraper-blade—that an expert carpenter would accept. We supplied to surveyors and others a very fine, strong line called China sea-grass line; it was used for suspending a plum bob, its fineness affording the minimum of agitation by wind currents. It was sold by the "catty," an Oriental unit of weight measurement amounting to about 1.33 pounds, and we got ours from Dame, Stoddard & Co., an old Boston house, which was, I believe, the only importer of it at the time. I recall also the stepladders from Paris, Maine—light yet stoutly braced and stable, the only brand of stepladders of such extra lengths as sixteen or eighteen feet on which the workman using it every day was willing to trust his safety.

I was reading an autobiography recently in which the narrator described his work in a stone quarry. His task, he wrote, was to hit with a sledge hammer the "steel drill" which his working partner was holding, and there were several allusions to this "steel drill." Since there must be few drills indeed that are not made of steel, I concluded as an old hardware man that what he meant was a star drill. Like the old popular songs of my youth, the terminology of the hardware business is still in my memory: the difference between a crowbar, a pinchbar, a wrecking bar, and—handiest of the lot—a crate opener; or the features of a night latch, a safety latch, a deadlock, and the several kinds of bolts; or screws: wood, lag, machine, set, cap, sheet metal, drive, dowel, and so on. What requires such a large capital outlay is the obligation to stock screws, for example, in a great variety of sizes—thickness and length—some of them in brass as well as iron or steel and, as in the case of wood screws, in two or three different styles of head. If the size and type called for is not available, the whole inventory is useless.

It happened that almost across the street from James Morton & Son Company was a news and magazine shop, a narrow, L-shaped little place operated by a ginger-haired Scotsman named McLaughlin. It still seems to me to have offered the most up-to-date and widely assorted periodicals I have found in any such place, and to the magazines my family provided at home I added the better pulps—*Adventure, Argosy, Blue Book, Green Book, Top-Notch,* and various oddities such as *The Railroad Man's Magazine* (pulp fiction about railroading), *Dog Fancier, The Pit Bull Terrier,* the outdoor magazines, and many others. I recall one, *Opportunity,* a thick, euphoric trade journal produced entirely for house-to-house salesmen, pitchmen, and small concessionaires ("Rush me details of Brown Bobby, the Greaseless Doughnut . . ."), which inspired me to find out whether high-grade German cutlery from James Morton & Son Company could be sold profitably by ringing doorbells, and I found out: it could not, although I sold about $30 worth of scissors one day to a woman simply by allowing her to recount to me the illnesses of her lifetime. I still have a top shelf filled with Nick Carter reprints which I used to buy from McLaughlin at two-for-a-quarter. My first leafing through of a copy of *Variety,* which I began to read regularly after a few samplings, was in McLaughlin's, and it was on account of my enjoyment of Sime Silverman's writing in *Variety* that I was able to get my first newspaper job years later, on *The Boston Herald.*

I was lucky, for reading resources, in having three Omaha friends who put all sorts of books at my disposal. The earliest was Frank Hanighen, a contemporary who became later on publisher of a Washington newsletter until his death in 1965, and with whom I exchanged books until I left Omaha. The second was a bookseller, Walter Hixenbaugh, a near neighbor with a reading taste that I found highly congenial, whose shelves held an ever-changing variety of first-rate books, new and old. It was from knowing Walter that I began collecting books in a small way and became a reader of most of the catalogues of the rare-book dealers in this country and England. I was obliged once, many years later, to make a speech—an activity of which I disapprove—to a large group of booksellers. I had observed that speakers usually try to get the audience warmed up and relaxed through an initial witticism, so I thought I would begin by describing myself as a bibliophile, or at any rate a former bibliophile. And what was a bibliophile? Why simply, ladies and gentlemen, one who buys rare books at very high prices and sells them later on at very low prices in order to buy more books at still higher prices. I was speaking from my own experience, and I was not at all prepared for the uproarious success of this mild little jape: the booksellers rocked with laughter, nudging each other, slapping their legs. This was going to be good, they could see, and I was horrified to find them all leaning forward intently, eager not to miss the bright line that they seemed sure was next on my tongue. Alas, I had expended my only witticism: the rest of my harangue was, *diminuendo*, a tedious account of the social insurance program, and I was gulping and halting as I watched the gusto of my audience give way to surprise and then to boredom.

The third of my book-lending friends was Harold Gifford, a marvelous personality—ophthalmologist, philanthropist, naturalist, first chairman of the Socialist Party in Nebraska, a humanitarian, and a stout friend. His library never failed to reward me with many books I would have otherwise missed, and he introduced me to the writings of such adventurers as Charles Finger, Harry Franck, R. B. Cunninghame Graham, and others. I recall going to see him one evening, jubilant, in my innocence, over the news that Governor Alvan T. Fuller had just appointed a committee of three, headed by A. Lawrence Lowell, to re-examine the record of the Sacco-Vanzetti Case. Old Dr. Gifford looked at me sympathetically. He knew a great deal more than I did about the convolutions of the Brahmin mind and the prestige that such a chairman as Lowell would enjoy with his committee. "I'm sorry," he said, "but those poor fellows are as good as dead."

School and college certainly did nothing to stimulate my reading. The College Board examinations covered two or three supposedly "good" books through which we were sweated, line by line: *Ivanhoe, Silas Marner,* and *Henry Esmond,* and it was not until I was in my thirties that I discovered Thackeray for myself and read with much satisfaction almost everything he had written. We were given, also, a kind of survey course in English literature, which consisted entirely of memorizing who had written what and when, in large quantities; it was information which had, if used guardedly, a certain utility in sparring with pundits at cocktail parties. For general orientation in the written word, the catalogues of the rare-book dealers were the most helpful to me.

Literary criticism has always been a scarce commodity in this country. Aside from the weekly reviews, which took themselves with great solemnity, I recall only H. L. Mencken's reviewing in the *Smart Set* and later in his *American Mercury* as being dependable and useful. Mencken put his arguments so forcefully, and his judgments seemed to me so valid, that I read his findings as eagerly as I did the books he was recommending. He confirmed many a suspicion for me when I was too young to trust my own opinion, and he broke ground for more new writers who were worth reading than anyone else in my experience. It was fashionable in his heyday to dismiss Mencken as show-off or a kind of professional bad boy; he was in the black books of most of the clergy, the Southerners, and the academics whose pretensions he described so entertainingly, and it was sophomoric, naïve to be taken in by him. I continue to think he was much needed during the years before the Great Crash of 1929, and I shall always feel grateful for the quality of his writing and editing at a time when the latest Conrad novel was received by other critics with as many hair-splittings and pros and cons as a new book from Jeffery Farnol or Harold Bell Wright.

I doubt that I ever became interested in the hardware business, and I am impressed by how many older men in one part of it or another used to warn me not to expect to enjoy myself. That might somehow come later, but it would have to be preceded by long periods of hard work and much unpleasantness. I may have seemed to these prophets an extremely callow and self-centered young man, intent only on enjoying himself, to have evoked this cautionary advice from so many of my elders. I think even my father was privately worried by how heartily I was attracted by pursuits quite unrelated to the business—travel, gambling, reading, good living—but the idea that I might find a way of making an occupation out of such tastes did not occur to him or to me. Of one thing I was certain: I was not enjoying my work. How to improve my position or to find an entirely different kind of work seemed quite beyond my capacity. The occupational future looked long and tiresome.

PART TWO

●●●

CHAPTER SEVEN

Trying to Write

SOME TIME in the forepart of 1926, I committed the extrava-
gance of buying a Corona portable typewriter. I believe I paid
about $65 for it. I had never used a typewriter, but I realized
that I would have to begin doing so if I expected anyone else—
especially a stranger-editor—to read what I wrote. It was time
to find out whether the notion that I might write successfully,
long germinating in the back of my head, could be valid or
whether it was merely a fantasy to be discarded. I had been
the editor of the school paper, *The Morristonian*, and I had
written a couple of burlesques that the Williams magazine,
The Purple Cow, published in the fall of 1916, but I had
made no attempt to write for the next ten years after that.

I cannot judge today how a series of rebuffs from editors
would have affected me in 1926. I know that I was genuinely
afraid of such a contingency, and I did not wish to risk, if I
could possibly avoid it, negations that might make me despair
of getting anywhere as a writer. The vehicles for my point of
view were none too numerous; the only one that seemed to
me just right for a trial spin was an iconoclastic little magazine
published in Girard, Kansas, *The Haldeman-Julius Monthly*.
Its proprietor was the purveyor of the Little Blue Books, which

were tiny boiled-down versions of thousands of classics, all in the public domain and not more than a sampling in each case of the book of the same title. The piece I wanted to write was about the absurdity of a certain kind of advertising, in which inexpensive and commonplace utilities were exhibited to the mass reader as being used and greatly admired by the very rich. One example, I recall, was a photograph of a liveried manservant bringing in an elaborate silver coffee service to a husband and wife in evening dress, amid much furniture and ornamentation, the whole being a boast in behalf of the rugs: garish colors and design imitating Oriental types only made of linoleum. Another depicted a man in a dinner jacket stoking a hot-air furnace of the cheapest type, the sort of unit a speculative builder would install in a jerry-built bungalow. I possessed a dozen or so such items, and I fortified about 900 words of prose with them one evening, titled it "The High Hat in American Advertising," and sent off to E. Haldeman-Julius, Editor.

Within the week I received a check for $10 for the piece. There was no covering letter with it, but a voucher indicated that it would be in print in about two months. I was enchanted. More money would have been welcome, but after all here was some money, real outside money, from a man who had never heard of me, in exchange for nothing more than a few remarks and opinions of my own. I had found out what I wanted to know: I was capable of selling something to *The Haldeman-Julius Monthly*, and I never sent anything there again. I found out, also, that working for two or three hours in the late afternoon or early evening would yield for me a fair quantity of copy, and that the work itself was quite satisfying as a distraction from my dead-end status in the hardware business.

I suppose every young writer would like to have a means of marketing his work in larger lots than one at a time. It was certainly easier for me to work for a reasonably hospitable outlet than to go through all the uncertainties and delays on each item that I sold. Any number of beginners send a single, fragmentary piece to the *Atlantic Monthly* over the years, with the suggestion that they could supply a long series of similar subjects or that we might wish to set up for them a monthly department or feature. At any rate, my own next venture was to write a series of short, hortatory articles, designed to inspire and cheer the retail hardware merchant. Most of what the trade journals published along these lines was virtually unreadable, and it seemed to be hard for their editors to find a contributor who knew what he was talking about and who could put it into ordinarily acceptable prose. At least I had the credential of being engaged in the business and writing from direct experience.

The problem was what posture I should assume. I was too young and with too little status for the role of sage and lawgiver, so I tried to envision a fictional character, but the minute this person began handing out advice and telling of his successes he was sounding like a vain and boastful bore. I dropped him after a couple of paragraphs, and it occurred to me that I could make my fictional character describe the wonderful exploits of a third party, without himself becoming the braggart. I was simply the omniscient narrator, reporting the conversation of my fictional character, and I decided to call him Pete Profit—good, genial old Pete Profit, loved and respected by hardware dealers throughout the land!—and the great lessons in salesmanship that I was propounding would be attributed by Pete Profit to his wonderful old partner. I need not add that the series was titled *Pete Profit's Partner*.

The partner was never named, but hovered over everything in the series like some allegorical presence: how to sell a very high-priced carving knife (by putting a razor edge on it and idly slicing thin ribbons from the edge of a newspaper page); a very high-priced coal scoop in large quantities to railroads,

111

power companies, and other large consumers (by demonstrating on the scales that it was lighter than other brands and then using it to bend and split a competing shovel into a shapeless bit of junk metal). The series took two of my evenings to write; I cannot recall whether there were three or five installments of it. I meant every word of it, and everything in it was indeed true: the kind of people who like to browse in a hardware store did buy the wondrous knife; the shovel was actually that good. The reason the series was so easy to write, I realized years later, was the same reason why James Morton & Son Company was on the wane: we sold only the best of everything, and our customer was presumably a professional, so that a housewife in need of an ordinary nail hammer would have to buy from us the David Maydole hammer that all the carpenters used or else find a cheaper hammer in some other shop.

I sent off the series to the editor of the principal trade journal, Llew S. Soule of *Hardware Age*, with a short letter on our business letterhead. He sent me a telegram a few days later: he liked the material, and how much did I want for it? I had no idea of what to ask or what he usually paid, but I told him he could have it for $40 an installment, to which he agreed. He gave the series a good play in his magazine, with black and white drawings of Pete Profit, who did not seem to me to look quite as opulent as he should have. I could not tell what my father thought about all this. I know he was pleased, but he never read the trade journals, and there was no way of foreseeing what I could do from that point on. I was no longer interested in writing for *Hardware Age* anyhow, and I never sent them another line. A new vista suddenly disclosed itself to me.

Morristown School was still sending me two or three times a year a newsletter to alumni. It was stirring news to read that Stephen Durant Hurlbut, who had gone to the school and was secretary of it while I was there, was joining the editorial staff of *Sportsman,* a new and very handsome monthly established in Boston by Richard E. Danielson and Christian A. Herter. Hurlbut was perhaps ten years older than I was, an extraordinarily good-looking man who could have served as the model for hats and all else in the Brooks Brothers advertisements. All the boys in the school agreed that his wardrobe was quite the finest we had ever seen, and I still recall the easy-going correctness of his appearance on all occasions, a tall, slim figure with a quiet affability that we all enjoyed.

Sportsman was very high style indeed, intended to appeal to the sort of people who maintained big country places with stables and kennels, kept ocean-going yachts, supported the horse shows and point-to-point races, and bought the Duesenbergs. It could hardly have been launched at a worse time, for it was only about three years later that the market crashed, and half-million-dollar yachts went begging at $20,000, but its proprietors gamely kept it in print until the late 30's, when the long Depression and the prospect of war put an end to it. It was a large turning point in my own affairs in the mid-20's.

Since there was no sport in which I could have stood as anything like an expert or commentator, I had some trouble in hitting on a subject to try out on Steve Hurlbut. I had read all the early issues of *Sportsman,* usually with some annoyance at what seemed excessively supercilious or snobbish attitudes on the part of the contributors, and I found myself quite offended by an article laying out the prospects for the next Maryland point-to-point race and what the Right People would be doing on that occasion. I undertook a burlesque of the piece, a similarly haughty, high-society presentation of great things to come at a hypothetical "sporting carnival" in Kansas —a program of bucolic competitions such as corn-husking, spitting at a mark, a greased-pig chase, and such. It was all *très snob* and overly affirmative. I recall only one line of it: "A regatta is planned, provided boats can be obtained and there is any water in Muddy River. . . ." I titled it "With Quid, Pig, and Mitten." On reading it over, some thirty years later, in Richard Danielson's file of *Sportsman*, I must confess I found it very funny. In any case, it brought me a pleasant letter from Steve and a check for $60.

During the next few months I sold *Sportsman* a lighthearted account of the long pack trip my wife and I took in the Wyoming Rockies in 1921, and a burlesque of *The Autobiography of Bobby Jones,* an "as-told-to" opus by his golfing mentor, O. B. Keeler.

The pack trip was a headlong flight from the ragweed season in Omaha and in its way something of a model of getting the maximum results from the minimum expenditure. Even in those days, an outfit of a dozen or so pack horses called for a couple of guides and cost $50 or $60 a day, far more than we could afford for a stay of two or three months. We worked out an arrangement with Irving Larom, the proprietor of the Lazy–JD, at Valley, Wyoming, surely the most delightful dude ranch in the West, that provided saddle horses and camping equipment for $10 a day, and two guides and a dozen pack horses for $150 for taking us out and setting up a base camp for us, and another $100 for bringing us back. The return would require only four or five horses, since most of our stores would have been consumed during the interval. What we gained, in effect, was eighty days of wilderness life, with all the excitement of being entirely on our own, for about a fourth the cost of keeping on the move with a big outfit. I had enough details to support a publishable article, but I have never felt at ease in trying to write the straightforward, objective, informative sort of piece, and the Jones-Keeler burlesque was a much more satisfying kind of project; its publication prompted me to try another burlesque, which proved to have a profound influence in fixing my course over the next forty years.

114

I should break off here briefly to explain that my main goal at this time was to be a newspaper columnist. I got nowhere with the Omaha *World-Herald*, where I tried to get a job as a news reporter or a columnist—occasionally, regularly, or on any basis at all. I finally started delivering to the editor a full column every day, in what I conceived to be a proper final form, for six days a week, to publish or throw away as he saw fit. I kept this up for about two months but received only mild commendations, polite evasions, and no publication. I would have gone to work for the *World-Herald* in any capacity, but they would have me in none. I still do not know why this was so; I had many friends on the staff, but I can only conclude that the management at the *World-Herald* regarded me as either a businessman—or a dilettante, or, worse, as having lived too much under the influence of The East.

But the next burlesque for *Sportsman* created other preoccupations. It was a little treatise, based on the mighty-hunter sort of article about big game in various parts of the world—what dear old Stephen Leacock used to sum up as "Every man his own hero"—that *Sportsman* and all the outdoor magazines were publishing. *Sportsman* had only just published one, and I was sure they would appreciate the point that I was trying to make. I titled it "How to Write a Big Game Article" and sent it off hopefully. Up to this point I had sold everything that I had sent out.

Steve Hurlbut responded a few days later. The big-game article was not for *Sportsman*, he wrote me, and if I kept on with my burlesques of sports, I would be taking the bread out of their mouths. But it did happen that Messrs. Danielson and Herter were jointly publishing and editing another magazine in Boston, a weekly review called *The Independent*, where my article would be most welcome. The pay was smaller, but the weekly would afford me a more frequent market.

This was great news. I was troubled by the scarcity of subjects for *Sportsman;* a weekly review would take in almost any subject or vein. I had never tried the *Nation* or *New Republic,* which were plainly addressed to a readership considerably beyond my reach. *The Independent* looked like a great opportunity. I began casting about for a formula that would afford me a regular weekly page in it—the dream of the tyro, and here now a chance to make it come true.

The scheme that I developed was no more than that of a causerie; it might deal with one subject or with several within the length of a page; it would not be committed to comedy or any particular mood and style, but the general tone would be on the light side. I wrote a prospectus and ten or fifteen examples of what I regarded as suitable content, and sent them off to *The Independent.* Every few days later, for a couple of weeks more, I sent more items, long and short. I did not care how the page might be signed, feeling sure in my egocentric ignorance that virtuosity would triumph over anonymity, in contrast to the more experienced political opinion that holds, "I don't care what you say about me but be sure to spell my name right." For a title I had what I still think was a fairly sound tag for the kind of stuff I was trying to write: "If You Know What I Mean . . ."

I don't believe *The Independent* sent me any word at all about the proposal for two weeks or more. Then one day—I think this was late in 1927—came a telegram from Christian Herter: they had decided to try out my page, letter follows and so forth.

The gust of pleasure from the telegram overwhelmed me. From this point on, I would travel a boulevard of success. My troubles were over. I was a made man. I could escape not only from the hardware business but also from Omaha. We could live wherever we wished. Where did we wish? We did not know, but all this was ours to decide. I really believed that my occupational problem was solved for all time: hereafter, I would improve with experience, I should enjoy it more and more as it did improve. Hah!

"If You Know What I Mean . . ." got off a rather muddled start. I doubt, in retrospect, that the editors of *The Independent* were more sophisticated in their pursuits than I was in mine, for their opening gambit was to present the page as written by "The Unknown Sage of Omaha." As for many Bostonians, I was to learn later that there was something droll for them in the very name of Omaha or anyone living there, and the fact that their venerable review was actually publishing a page originating in Omaha was funny as all get-out in itself. But after a week or two of this prankishness, they realized that *The Independent* was not altogether at its best in ribbing its own stuff, and we settled down together without the horseplay. Occasionally I had a pleasant letter from Herter, and my regular correspondence was with Stewart Beach, the managing editor, who became a valued friend for all the years that followed and who went on to make a career for himself in Washington and New York.

●●

CHAPTER EIGHT

Escape to Massachusetts

I CONTINUED to work in the hardware store and to write in my spare time, but by the spring of 1928 we were firmly decided to leave Omaha and settle somewhere in the vicinity of Boston. We sold our house, put the furniture in storage, and in late June drove off to spend the summer in a little mountainside house at Evergreen, Colorado, overlooking Bear Creek Canyon. The house was owned by close friends of ours in Omaha, Conrad and May Young, and we ran a joint household, pooling and pro-rating expenses and having a marvelous time: the Youngs and their two children, my wife and I and our eight-year-old daughter Patricia. Clara Nosal, who had cooked for us for several years, did the cooking and came along with us in September when we set out to storm the publishing world of Boston. She came from a village in the Nebraska sugar-beet country; her parents were immigrants from Poland, and under my wife's guidance she became a virtuoso of really elegant cookery. She became so accomplished, in fact, that when she returned to the West in the spring of 1929, she opened a small boardinghouse in Council Bluffs, where one of her elderly guests, after enjoying her meals for three or four years, left her something like $200,000 on his death.

We stopped briefly in Omaha before leaving for Boston on Labor Day. I was saddened to leave my parents, but I am sure they were relieved to have me trying to follow a clearer course and with an outside chance of success, something not all apparent in the hardware business. My father had given me the family car at the beginning of the summer, a Cadillac sedan. It had taken some weathering during our summer in the mountains, but I had installed in it a rear-axle ratio of 3.70 to 1, which gave it a fairly high cruising speed on a long drive. It was the only car I have ever owned that was equipped with a condenser as a unit in a sealed water-cooling system so that steam from the radiator, if the engine overheated on a long climb, was condensed into water again and returned to the radiator. It enabled us to ascend the steep grades of the road up Pikes Peak without losing any water, indeed without stopping at all.

I say we left "for Boston," but the truth is that we had no real destination. There were four of us, with much luggage inside and on the running boards, and Harry, a Kerry blue terrier, and Tom, an Irish wolfhound. My own dog Dick, an English bull terrier, I left with Paul and Rachel Gallagher in Omaha. They admired him greatly. To me he seemed the only dog worth having, but he was far from the friends-making kind of accessory with which to settle down among strangers. The big hound was a gentleman at all times, the Kerry blue a clown. Our trip eastward was uneventful, and it was not until we reached a hotel in Fitchburg—of all places—that we began to think of a temporary destination.

Some friends at the University of Nebraska had given Hingham a high rating. It had everything: a seaside location near Boston, an unpretentious, easygoing community with a good layer of Old New England. We decided to deflect toward the southeast and see what Hingham was like. We reached Hingham at about 10:30 in the morning and stopped at a real estate office. We wanted a furnished house for the winter, possibly longer.

The old saw that it's always low tide when visitors come held good for us in Hingham. My recollection of the two hours we spent there is of mud flats, unattractive houses, and a bad lunch in a bad restaurant. It was a discouraging forenoon. I had spent two or three summers at Marblehead as a small boy in an old-time hotel on Marblehead Neck, the Nannepashemet, and I remembered it as a rocky shore and quite without mud flats. It was a Friday, very hot, and we could at least spend the weekend there and look around.

At midafternoon we were in the thick of one of Boston's celebrated traffic jams—child, dogs, luggage, and all—waiting for the drawbridge to close and let us through to Charlestown. But by the end of the day we were comfortably and inexpensively lodged in an old ramshackle hotel called the Boylston, on Marblehead Neck, which was operated in the summer season as an annex of the Eastern Yacht Club.

The next morning we found a real estate man and looked at some lovely houses, one of them tucked away at the water's edge at the end of a private lane where I should have been happy to spend the rest of my life, but everything was more than we could afford. We finally signed up for just the right place—still too expensive—on a knoll in the Clifton section of town. The sight and sound of the sea were irresistible, and through a telescope at a big window in the living room one could see the shipping traffic in the lower part of Boston harbor. Our greatest concern about the house was its gas furnace, but the gas company assured us that a special low rate for furnaces was in effect. The gas bill for the month of November was $125. The furnace gave a faintly audible puff each time the thermostat turned it on, a sound that I never heard without wincing through the rest of the winter. The summer

120

rental of the house for three months was three times the total we were paying for nine, so that our lease ended on June 15.

The page in *The Independent* was going along smoothly enough, and I had set up a book project which would occupy most of my working time for several months, editing and compiling an anthology from *Variety*. I needed a file of the paper to work on, and I hoped to be able to get one from Sime Silverman in New York, the owner and editor of *Variety*. My first obligation was to call at the office of *The Independent* and meet the editors who had given me so welcome a foothold in journalism.

The Independent and *Sportsman* offices, one and the same, were in a fine old brownstone house at 10 Arlington Street. Herter and Danielson shared a large office looking out over the Public Garden across the street, a pleasant view at any season of the year. They were both remarkably handsome, casually and elegantly turned out, and quite dissimilar: Herter was perhaps ten years the younger, very tall, spare, with rumpled brown hair and a great air of keenness and good humor; Danielson, then in his forties, looked very fit, ruddy, immaculate, with white hair and a small, closely trimmed white mustache, and his appearance never seemed to change in the almost thirty years that I knew him, even during long intervals of poor health. Beach, their general executive in editorial matters, was delightful, a soft-voiced, capable, well-informed chap of about my own age who I learned, alas, would soon be moving to New York. The fact was, Herter told me, that *The Independent* had just been taken over by *Outlook*, edited in New York by Francis Rufus Bellamy, but he hastened to assure me that I need have no concern about my page: Bellamy was very keen to keep it in the combined publication, which would be called *Outlook and Independent*. Stephen Hurlbut had left *Sportsman* and become an importer of English antique furniture and

121

silver, with a shop on Charles Street that he subsequently transferred to New York.

Bellamy, when I called at his office a few days later in New York, raised the rate for my weekly page from $30 to $40, which was encouraging. Sime Silverman, whom I saw several times in the next year, was skeptical about a *Variety* anthology, but he was so astonished on learning that I did not expect him to subsidize me that he promptly shipped me a bound file of *Variety.* I worked throughout the winter trying to put together the items that seemed to me worth anthologizing, but the result was a sad hodgepodge. I took it down to New York in the spring and left it with Clifton Fadiman, who was then an editor at Simon and Schuster. I knew it would be rejected, and when it was, in a polite letter asking what I wished to do with the manuscript, I never answered the question. Sime was right: it was a difficult project for anyone, and I was too inexperienced to come anywhere near bringing it off. I kept on working at it long after I began to sense its failure, as if the work itself were somehow justifying my effort to earn a living in Marblehead.

Outlook and Independent began dropping behind in paying me in the first months of 1929. The magazine was in trouble, and I was not surprised to get a letter from Bellamy in the early spring that he was discontinuing my page. It behooved me to get on a payroll, and I went in to see Robert Choate, who was then managing editor and later became publisher of *The Boston Herald.* He was a friend of Herter's, who had shown him some of my writing, but he did not respond with an offer of any sort when I asked him for a job on the news staff.

Variety's file contained a particularly amusing series by Sime Silverman about a New York confidence man who dropped in on him from time to time to boast of his latest swindles. The man may be still alive, for all I know, and I shall give him the name of Spelvin Hunt. He was a notorious figure in midtown New York, so much so that he was obliged to turn to Philadelphia and Boston for new victims. It was about a week after I saw Choate that the *Herald* carried a short story on page one reporting the disappearance of the promoter who had put on an "Irish Fair" in Boston Garden. The Fair had occupied the Garden for several days, but the promoter had vanished without troubling to pay the performers he had engaged or even the rent for use of the Garden, and all the gate receipts seemed to have gone with him. The promoter was one Spelvin Hunt, of New York.

It was a drab story, with overtones of outrage and some local chagrin at the misbehavior of a New Yorker, obviously written and edited by people who had never heard of Spelvin Hunt and Sime's hilarious accounts of him. I went quickly through the best half-dozen stories about him that I had marked in the file, typed out a follow-up story quoting Sime, and took it in to William Gavin, the night city editor of the *Herald*. Gavin telephoned me that evening that they would be running the story the next morning, and he asked me to go to New York and try to find and interview Spelvin Hunt.

I took the eight o'clock train the next morning and hurried over to *Variety's* office on West 46th Street. Sime was much amused by the Irish Fair episode, and he turned me over to Lester Jacob, one of his advertising salesmen, who he said would know where Spelvin Hunt would be found if he had returned to New York—but this was most unlikely, Sime thought. Spelvin Hunt was undoubtedly elsewhere, waiting for things to cool down.

Jacob took me to three or four speakeasies and offices in the neighborhood, but our man had not been around for a week or more. Finally he introduced me to Spelvin Hunt's brother, who might provide me with some kind of story for the *Herald*. I did not really expect the brother to have anything to say for publication, which shows how little I knew about midtown New York. Some brotherly concern seemed more likely to make him prefer to keep quiet, I thought, and I was dazzled by the violence of the tirade Spelvin's brother loosed against him. The latter, it transpired was running a small-time booking agency and had actually supplied a few musicians and entertainers for the Irish Fair. I wrote down verbatim everything that he was saying and it all got better and better; the more he said, the madder he got. He was even out of pocket for the rail fares of the acts he had supplied, to say nothing of salary owed them. I filed the story with Western Union at around 7:00 P.M., took The Owl to Boston, and was pleased to see the story on page one the next morning. I turned in an expense account of something like $28, the lowest, Choate told me gleefully some years later, ever presented by a *Herald* staff man for a trip to New York and back.

Gavin telephoned me to come into the office the next day. "There's a woman in Boston," he said, "who is trying to set up shop as a wrestling promoter. It might make an odd sort of story." Those were the only instructions that Gavin gave me on the story that developed; their brevity and blandness proved to be quite useful some years later when the million-dollar libel suit that the story produced came to trial. In the office, Gavin introduced me to Fred Brine, the *Herald's* courthouse reporter, who would take me to the woman's flat in the Back Bay. Brine presented me to the woman, who was expecting us, and left.

I asked Sime Silverman one day to define for me the slang word "magimp" as used by *Variety's* Jack Conway in reviewing a melodrama. Sime was stumped, but he thought Jack's widow, who was working in the office, might know. "Oh yes," she said, after meditating on the question for a moment. "A magimp is she's keeping him." Something like that seemed to obtain between the woman I went to see and the unsuccessful promoter that she had been financing. She felt that the wrestling "trust" headed by the late Paul Bowser had persuaded the press to belittle her friend's wrestling matches, with the result that she was losing considerable money on them. Worse, I gathered that the magimp's affections had cooled as her financial support diminished. She was now out for revenge, and on her dining-room table, under an old-time Tiffany glass center light, were stacked the documents to get it for her. That, in brief, was the synopsis as we sat down at the table and began examining the material.

The woman's search for evidence was simplicity itself. She subscribed to a clipping service, asking for any sports stories about Gus Sonnenberg, who was Bowser's reigning "heavyweight champion of the world" at the time. All Sonnenberg's barnstorming matches in the small towns of the hinterland were heavily publicized well in advance, so that she was able to make her next move before the match was held: she sent a one-dollar bill to the local postmaster in such towns, asking him to send her in return any advertising placard about the match having photographs of the participants. A great pile of such placards was on her dining-room table, with sheaves of news stories and photographs of the participants.

As everyone came to know, Gus was wrestling the same opponent several times each week on his tours, all the matches were advertised as "championship" contests in which Gus' title was at stake, the only change from one match to the next being a new name for his opponent. The clips and the placards made the whole arrangement all too clear, including the venality of virtually all the sports writers and editors concerned. It was marvelous to read that Gus was wondering what manner of man his opponent would prove to be, and to read the same story in another paper published a few days earlier or later, the only difference being the opponent's name.

I picked out an assortment of the clips and placards, took

125

them down to Marblehead, wrote the story, and turned the story and the supporting items over to Gavin the next day. It was a preposterous set of facts, disclosed at just the right moment, for the Boston papers had been earnestly building up a new world's championship match with Sonnenberg which was scheduled for a few weeks later. I believe the sports editor of the *Herald* was given no advance hint that the story was in the making; he accosted me the next day in the *Herald* office where I was working on a follow-up about Sonnenberg's "championship" match at Dartmouth College, where Gus had played football as an undergraduate. Gus' boon to dear old Alma Mater in this case was to wrestle the same ringer, under what name for the latter I do not recall, and to pass it all off as a bona-fide contest. The *Herald's* sports editor obviously did not approve of the story or me, but it had all gone far beyond any backtracking that he could do. By the time the libel suit filed by Bowser and Sonnenberg was heard some years later, wrestling was taken as no more than rough-and-tumble entertainment, and all I offered as a witness was that I wrote the story and that no one had instructed me in how to write it.

Choate told me, after the Sonnenberg story, that I could come to work as a news reporter and to draw a week's pay for the work I had done. This seemed good news indeed, until I found that the week's pay was $35. I objected so strenuously that Choate raised me to $45 a couple of weeks later. My wife and our daughter Patricia went to Meriden, New Hampshire, to spend the summer, and I moved into a lodging house on Beacon Hill. In spite of the bad pay, I thought I had at least made a start. As for the work itself, few jobs are more entertaining for a young man—although I was thirty years old by this time and a late starter for the kind of work I was doing—than that of news reporter on a morning paper in a metropolitan area.

We moved into an apartment in Cambridge at the end of the summer. In December, 1929, our younger daughter, Cynthia, was born and I was able to find a job on *The Boston Evening Transcript*. From this point on, I assured my family, everything would really open up for us: our troubles were over.

●●

CHAPTER NINE

The Boston Evening Transcript

WHEN I went to work for *The Boston Evening Transcript* as a news reporter at the beginning of 1930, it seemed to me a wonderfully good break. It had taken me almost eight years to disentangle myself from the hardware business. Yet, with barely a year of newspapering behind me, I was on the staff of this celebrated sheet. True, its circulation was somewhere around 38,000, but many of us, in office conjectures, felt that this figure could be boosted to 40,000—perhaps even 45,000—if we all pitched in on the news side. The fact that our circulation was slightly junior to that of evening papers in Passaic, New Jersey, Canton, Ohio, and Elmira, New York impressed none of us. All we knew about circulation was that the *Transcript*, in some mysterious way, could get along without it.

The Depression was just at its onset. I doubt that any of us understood at the time why the stock market crash of a few months earlier did in fact mean the inevitable end of the paper. Our general reaction was that things were tough for the moment, so tough that they could only change for the better. Yet the real situation was that the *Transcript* had depended almost exclusively on financial advertising announcing new issues of all sorts of securities. On this category of display space, the *Transcript's* rate was approximately the same as that of the New York *Daily News,* which had a circulation more than twenty-five times as large as ours. The paper might have lived comfortably on this income had it continued, with relatively high revenues and the low production costs of a small circulation. But when financial advertising stopped, as it did, the paper had to begin suddenly to live on its fat.

At the beginning of 1930, in spite of the portents, the *Transcript's* news staff was far from pessimistic. There was a vague legend in the city room that whenever circulation shot up again to the 45,000 mark, the department stores would suddenly reinstate their advertising in the *Transcript.* The legend had a strange quality of reality for us; it was almost as if a committee representing the department stores would meet on a certain day, summon our advertising manager, and bestow on him a packet of lavish contracts. Meanwhile, as we were given to imagining, the committee was watching closely our circulation figures, awaiting only the reassurance of that additional five or seven thousand readers. At the time of my arrival, the paper was losing not more than $500 a day. My own part in this deficit was a wage of $55 a week and an expense account that ranged between $3 and $4 a month. The department store situation, we felt, was temporary, even though it had obtained for decades. It was bound to improve and eventually to bring a general lift in city-room salaries. This would be especially true in the case of later arrivals, such as myself, who naturally received less pay than the veterans. It was one of the very first inequalities which would be ironed out just as soon as the department stores saw the light.

Working conditions at the *Transcript* were generally regarded by Boston newspapermen as ideal. The first of its three editions on weekdays closed at 10:30 A.M., and the local staff did not have to report for work until 8:15 A.M. Unlike morning-paper

129

people, we were able to sleep nights. We had Sundays off, closed at 1:15 P.M. on Saturdays. We were allowed as much as fifteen or twenty minutes for lunch. If a man appeared five minutes late of a morning, in some instances he was not even admonished.

Practically everything in the *Transcript* was in a department. We had one called "Patriotic and Historical"; another was "The Churchman Afield"; and we had a big one entitled "Genealogical." Even our sports page was subdivided, with specialists who covered nothing but golf, or yachting, or horses and dogs.

So great was the degree of specialization that almost anything remotely relating to a department was handed over to its proprietor for expert treatment. Every year, for instance, a considerable number of Bostonians would be announced as ticket holders in the Irish Sweepstakes, and the news staff was sent out among them to find out what the winners would do with the money. These stories at times were odd and amusing, and the Boston Irish must have bought enough Sweepstakes tickets over the years to build hospitals for most of the Western world. But no matter how numerous or queer the stories, the disposition of them was always assigned to the horse-and-dog editor, on the theory that these winnings were resulting from a horse race, the Grand National or the Derby. Ordinary news judgments confronted by such a circumstance, so the reasoning went, would be incompetent.

I have forgotten some of the nomenclature, but there were also departments dealing with schools and colleges, women's clubs, banks and real estate, necrology, and so on. By and large, the proprietor of one of these departments did nothing else. He was a specialist, an expert—indeed, he was known as an "editor," and in dealings with the outside world would casually refer to himself as "one of the editors of *The Boston Evening Transcript*." In this sense, the paper must have had twenty or thirty editors. Their day was more leisurely than that of the news staff; they seemed to have to do a great deal of reading in the office, thumbing through the trade journals of their specialty, boning up on the latest caper among Sealyham breeders or road-builders. Occasionally one would seize shears and a pot and paste up, verbatim, a long release from a press agent or an advertising agency, and this would appear intact a few days later in the larger Wednesday or Saturday edition. Probably no other paper ever brought such joy and astonishment to publicists, and one can only imagine their reactions at finding the whole handout in a Saturday *Transcript* without even its lead rewritten, let alone abridged.

These "editors" were obliged to spend considerable time away from the office, at meetings and conventions. They traveled widely, but the technique was usually the same, and the signed story, arriving in great lumps of Western Union copy, usually bore a strange similarity to the mimeographed material which had already reached the office as third-class mail, advance copy.

I had been on the *Transcript* staff for about two weeks when I finally asked one of the other news reporters about one of the hard-reading editors.

"What does that fellow do?" I inquired.

The answer was brief but definitive: "If it isn't banks, he doesn't do it."

With so many desks occupied by editors, the *Transcript* maintained no rewrite staff as such. There would not have been room for one, and I dare say it would have seemed a needless expense. The news staff, consequently, did its own legwork and its own writing. If the story were in town and the hour suitable, the staff man rushed back to the office and wrote his story. He had to write his own heads, incidentally, and usually had to decide how big a head the story deserved. He then read copy on himself and as often as not popped the story,

131

without further reading by anyone, into a tube to the com-
posing room. It was up to the make-up man upstairs, then, to
shuffle things around and locate them as he saw fit. If the
reporter was particularly attracted by his story, he would mark
it "Page One." If he had doubts about its future, he would
even add "Must." In this way, the city editor undoubtedly
found a lot of news in the paper each evening which he had
never seen before. We were not altogether sure who the managing editor was at any given moment, but the same would
have been true in his case. I don't intend to imply that we
had any great turnover in managing editors but rather that
the title and function were for some years at any rate, a matter
of conjecture.

Again for reasons obscure to me, this somewhat informal
system seemed to work out happily enough. In the early part
of the day, a certain amount of copy was read and pondered,
but along toward closing time, the common practice was to
railroad as much of it as seemed necessary. This gave the city
editor an abundance of free time, so that he was able to keep
a vigilant eye on how long the news staff took for lunch.

Apart from the assortment of editors, the *Transcript's* news
staff included the normal list of beat men—city hall, water-
front, police headquarters, and such—a wholly unpredictable
string of suburban correspondents, many of whom were un-
heard from for months on end, and a hard core of a half-
dozen or so writing reporters. We were all virtuosos, possessed,
in the face of constantly diminishing evidence to support it, by
the belief that all Boston, and much of the outside world, depended breathlessly each day on what we were about to write.
Whereas this may have been true of press agents and public
relations artificers, who would have been foolish indeed to
omit clipping the first edition, in which so much of their "advance" copy was served forth intact, I doubt that other parts

of the paper produced quite the impact on the reader that the writing of them did on us.

The average age of our circulation must have been the highest in the land, but we plugged along at the run of the news without realizing that the department of "Recent Deaths" was probably the hottest piece of reading matter in the paper for most of the customers. When the *Transcript* finally suspended publication in 1941, I overheard a dialogue between two elderly Bostonians which afforded a fair hindsight, it seems to me, on how we had been doing. *The Christian Science Monitor,* a paper celebrated for its reluctance to mention death from any cause, was falling heir, temporarily, to some of the *Transcript's* circulation, and the two Bostonians were comparing notes.

The conversation, as they reached for their evening papers, went:

"Too bad about the *Transcript.*"

"Great paper."

"What are you reading now?"

"Globe."

"I'm trying the *Monitor.*"

"Well, I tried the *Monitor* awhile ago, but I didn't like it. Couldn't tell who's dead or anything."

I must pull up for a moment at this point to explain that the *Transcript's* interest in necrology as something calling for the maximum journalistic effort was matched only by the attention it paid to football and the stock market. Nothing threw the city room into so much high-speed sleuthing and telephoning as a first-rank bereavement. A system of research into maiden names, grandparents, undergraduate clubs at Harvard, Junior League, Sewing Circle, and funeral arrangements was immediately set in motion. Anyone passing our two telephone booths could tell by the unctuous tones of the reporter inside that he was talking to a newly bereft relative of an influential

133

corpse. A bedside manner beyond reproach, it became a stunt of the first order, part of the office repertory of conversational histrionics; the man who could get the most spuriously funereal or excessively sympathetic note into the clichés of the occasion rightly counted himself an artist, esteemed by all.

Great lumps of trivial detail which no other paper would have dreamed of publishing thus fortified the *Transcript's* obits. We were especially interested in the deaths of Harvard graduates and anyone with early New England ancestry, and this latter category would embrace at full length even those families which were no longer rich. When a really big death came along, someone who met all the tests—old family, Harvard, still rich—the response would be about the same as to a general conflagration. Other prominent citizens would be telephoned and induced to say for publication that they deeply regretted the death; our obituary editor would turn to; the male society editor of the *Transcript* would put in one of his rare appearances in the city room to see that no reference work lay unconsulted; other news projects were sidetracked as the pursuit of funeral arrangements was loosed. After a fury of telephoning, typing, pasting, and scanning, the obit would be sent along, the most lavish journalistic compliment the deceased had ever received. The extent of the obit was bound to surprise even the most infatuate relatives and friends of its subject.

If the *Transcript* went to town on a death, it outdid itself on a funeral. Whereas the death might have turned up first in the morning papers, most funerals were held during the *Transcript's* working hours. Here was another chance to demonstrate the solid virtues of an evening sheet, to teach the A.M.s a lesson in how to clean up on a big story and leave nothing for the next day. It was not uncommon for us to send more staff to a funeral than to a murder trial, even though church services and burial seemed to have been worked out, as a general thing, on a fairly stable basis—that is, without disorders, arrests, or whatever it was that we expected to have happen at the obsequies which called for the vigilance of a smart news staff. It was no particular trick to get the names of the clergy, pallbearers, and the musical program over the phone, but we covered the funerals just the same to make sure that no slip-ups occurred. We spent most of our time outside, leaning up against churches, although in a fit of tenacity I once elbowed my way into a sort of minstrel's gallery at the funeral of a prominent banker and market rigger and sat in the middle of a bosomy quartet of female vocalists. A variation of this kind was well regarded by the rest of the city staff, in that it was hard to do and had, at the same time, a certain useless quality which appealed to all of us.

I believe it would be fair to take our obits as representing the ideal *Transcript* story. The obit was always too long, for the executives held that the longer the story, the harder the reporter had worked, an end in itself. A short story could not be so desirable as a long one, since it meant that the reporter had been frittering away his time in lunchrooms or worse—a correct estimate, I must add, since we did go to almost any lengths to get out of the office for a few hours.

The obit had a great deal less standing with other papers in Boston. This enabled the *Transcript* to harvest richly in the field of obituaries and to feel at ease in an appreciation of news values which other editors did not have enough sense to comprehend. The obit was authoritative, exhaustive, and uninteresting. It required more work than it was worth, and it was a story which other papers usually managed to do without. It was, in sum, what we used to call a "technical scoop."

It sounds absurd to say that the *Transcript* had a commercial interest in funerals, that what we published under "Recent Deaths" was by way of being a "reader," like one of the pasted-up stories describing plans for the regional convention of Frigidaire salesmen. I am sure that none of our executives, consciously, expected the legatees of a *Transcript* death to start an advertising campaign in the paper as a result of the handsome obit. But I could not escape the notion, watching so many pallbearers shouldering their burdens, that an excellent reason must underlie our interest. Wiser heads than mine had figured it out, and I was willing to give it a whirl. Although it was hard for me to see what use the beneficiaries of a Boston trust might want to make of our advertising columns, the answer might lie somewhere in the overlapping and mysterious intricacies of high finance. Perhaps the deceased himself had been the stumbling block, cherishing an old prejudice against the *Transcript* and preventing his associates from giving us a little business. Perhaps even now they were re-examining, in the light of our unique performance, their earlier judgments of newspaper media and rates. With the old man out of the way, a fresh approach was possible. New ties could be cemented in sorrow or in relief or whatever, and things would pick up again for the *Transcript.*

As I say, no one formally enunciated any such motives. I doubt if I could have discerned them at the time, yet they are perfectly plain to me today, and they offer almost the only explanation of why so many dissimilar people worked so hard for so little at projects so completely wide of the mark. Only good could follow such drudgery, we felt. But like the department stores, the heirs and successors never did get around to laying it on the line. A friend or a flunky of the deceased with some literary flair or reputation would favor us with a memoir for the editorial page a week or two later, but that was about all. We even made a final stab at the proceedings in probate court, reporting faithfully the public bequests—the sums to be shared equally by the Animal Rescue League, the New England Home for Little Wanderers, the Boston Seaman's Friend Society, the Boston Society for the Care of Girls, the New England Anti-Vivisection Society, Trinity Church and such—and the story always ended: "The residuary estate is to be held in trust for the widow during her lifetime. . . ." It was not that we actually expected to be mentioned in the will, yet my own vague impression was that the testator would have put the *Transcript* down on his list if he had only realized our great need.

A horde of charitable organizations preyed upon the *Transcript* in its latter years. No scheming merchant, if we had been blessed with the advertising of local retailers, would have coerced the paper into so many puffs, endorsements, and so much general publicity as these welfare organizations unblushingly exacted from the *Transcript*. True, they did carry paid announcements in the paper each week, but, I suspect, at nominal rates, and for every line of what they were buying, they obtained without charge truly fantastic hospitality for their press releases. Like the fifty-fifty hash of rabbit and horse, one rabbit for one horse, the deal amounted to a half-column of free space for every line of advertising. It became another of the despairing stunts with which the city staff idled away its time to see who could get into the paper verbatim the longest and worst press releases from this swarm of vultures.

Here again was a curious motivation. One would not expect a staff genuinely striving for the paper's success to cripple its pages with such pitiful rubbish. In this case, the whole thing was a queer, reverse English attempt to rid ourselves of the city editor.

As I have said, the news staff was an oddly assorted group, but it had a common characteristic, the blend of ignorance, egotism, and enthusiasm with which each of us viewed the *Transcript* and our own part in it. We were going to save the paper in spite of itself, and most of our momentum was spent on that hapless functionary, the city editor, who was in fact the only executive with whom we had to deal. So firmly was the discipline of our relationship fixed that none of us ever gave him a flat refusal or denounced him to his face, and it seems unlikely that he would have known what we were talking about had we tried to straighten him out. He was the inheritor of the attitudes which he applied to us, but we detested him and, again in our innocence, were sure that, given his head, he would commit some supreme folly which would eliminate him. Thus, when it came to letting a handout from the Anti-Vivisection Society drivel along without the touch of a pencil, we counted it a bitter medicine for the paper but one which might at least cure the *Transcript* of its city editor. Someone was bound to see the stuff and complain.

I recall putting up a whole treatise, unabridged, from the M.S.P.C.A. on how to boil a live lobster without causing it pain, although the biological authority for the recipe was really no more than the fiat of the Society's publicity man. If anyone really cares, the method, as I remember it, was to start the lobster off in lukewarm water and bring it slowly to the boil. This is not only at direct variance with the approved water's-edge theory of beginning with boiling water, but if you stop to think of it, it sounds like a prolongation and refinement of whatever discomfort the lobster experiences. The press release explained that the lukewarm water made the lobster groggy and that it yielded up the spirit hardly aware that anything unusual was going on. I have mentioned this press release at times in trying to explain the *Transcript*, but it was always taken to be mere facetiousness on my part. All I can say is that I am willing to bet anyone that a deadpan telephone inquiry or visit to the M.S.P.C.A. will bring, even today, an official written instruction on how to boil a live lobster without hurting it enough to give the Society grounds for action. (I have never seen any similar release from the Society with respect to oysters.)

I worked for the *Transcript* almost seven years. In five of

138

them we were each presented with a turkey on Thanksgiving, or rather with a turkey order on some market. In the sixth there was no turkey order. We took three pay cuts—a 10, a 20, and a 40 per cent reduction; it may have been two 20's instead of the 40. At any rate, I left the paper in the summer of 1936 on a Saturday afternoon. With one stratagem or another, by running my legs off for six and a half years, I was getting only $10 a week less than when I had started.

●●●

CHAPTER TEN

The Transcript:
"Our Kind of People..."

"OUR KIND OF PEOPLE" was a phrase often heard in the city room of *The Boston Evening Transcript*. It was used by the city editor—the one we disliked—with an air of certitude, as if he and whoever was talking with him understood each other perfectly on who were our kind of people. It was like speaking of an organized and identifiable elite, with a secret grip and recognition signal of its own. To be included in the mutual acceptance of such a term as "our kind of people" and thereby become a party to the city editor's petty snobbery was irritating to a news reporter, and the words were parroted by the staff with gusto. "Anything to do with our kind of people?" someone would ask as a reporter came in from a story.

The answer to this question was largely pantomime. The reporter would solemnly nod an affirmative and assume a glassy-eyed, mindless expression, beginning to hum an off-key air, at the same time rapidly flapping down his lower lip with a forefinger, like a man playing a jew's-harp. These actions were supposed to denote, and they did so most effectively, a state of feeble-mindedness, with overtones of nameless tendencies in almost any direction. The story would prove to be a bit of piffle, probably no more than supplying the l. to r. names, with a head and legend, for a photograph of some rummage-sale chairman and her aides, but they had been our kind of people (*bibble-bibble-bibble* . . .).

The *Transcript* rarely sent out a photographer without a reporter to identify persons in the picture, and this created a fabulous sort of misery-loves-company day's work with Frank Colby, our photographer. Frank's son, Warren, was our only other photographer, but it was Frank whom the city editor sent on what he regarded as the best assignment; i.e., a small group of "our kind of people" about to hold a meeting, or just having held one, in the interests of some queer charity or cultural pursuit. (Releases from the Browning Society were always published verbatim in the *Transcript*, and so were those from the Anti-Vivisection Society, for the latter always ended with the same two sentences, long favorites with the staff: "Tea was served. John Orth rendered several selections on the piano.")

Colby was around sixty, corpulent but able to stay on the run with his competition. His blue suit was spotted with chemicals, and the old felt hat which he pulled down over his ears and his vast threadbare ulster made no concessions to appearances. He had never taken a drink in his life and he rarely used rough language, but such was his general effect, often aggravated by two or three days' beard, that most strangers dealt timidly with him. An-old style Yankee individualist, whose forebears once farmed it on the bank of the Charles River in Cambridge, Frank was something of an expert on furniture and china. He detested the police and all in uniform; most of the bench, he felt, was corrupt; the only people he disliked more than police were the officious banquet and catering flunkies who, misled by Frank's hat and ulster, failed to accord him the respect which he felt was due any representative of *The Boston Evening Transcript*. Frank once bumped a New York photographer, with a swing of his heavy Graflex,

141

from a float into Marblehead harbor for disparaging words about the *Transcript*.

A story Frank was fond of retelling, and which we were always glad to hear on account of its blow-off line, had to do with his triumph over an old enemy, a caterer's head waiter who removed, while Frank was out of the room for a moment, the camera and tripod Frank had set up at a wedding reception. The wedding in this case was what the *Transcript's* male society editor used to call "an event of social consequence"; all concerned, but especially the bride's mother, were distinctly "our kind of people," and it was to her that Frank hastened to tell his troubles. Her reaction could scarcely have been more to Frank's taste. Before his entire staff she led the caterer's man—by the ear, one might have thought, to hear Frank tell it—to the corner where camera and tripod were relegated. "She pointed to my camera, leaned up there in the corner," Frank's story concluded, "and she says to this flunky so that everybody could hear: 'Who, may I ask, *done* THAT?' "

As the principal victim of the city editor's wooing of the Back Bay and Beacon Hill, Colby had all sorts of ways of adding self-entertainment to an unworthy assignment. The people who strive to get pictures of themselves into a newspaper are much the same anywhere, and after a quarter-century of dealing with them Frank could make them believe almost anything. The eagerness with which they accepted even his most nonsensical pronouncements about light and shadow and his purportedly *sotto-voce* consultations with the reporter on that subject was almost embarrassing.

There were none of today's cameras that "think for themselves" in Colby's kit. The flash bulb was imminent, but a tray of magnesium powder, which ignited with a boom and tended to shower a fine ash dust over its vicinity, was still the ordinary way of lighting a shot in the absence of sufficient daylight. Photography of professional quality was an arcane pursuit; the non-professional, listening to learned discussions of the lighting, "the back-ground," distances, and such, was quickly made to feel that this particular project would prove to be a hard one, if not all but impossible. What blighting effect, for instance, might a reflection from that mirror, or the glass door of that desk, have on the picture? How could one be sure?

The arrival of Colby and the *Transcript* reporter in a Beacon Hill drawing room usually plunged into a state of tension what had been up to that point a harmless morning coffee. Madame Chairman, in whose house the ladies were meeting, might even be looking about her with some complacency: a well-waxed, polished scene, the portraits, good mahogany, silver, the Kerman that Uncle Fred had left them—some of these might appear to advantage in the photograph, or so she might reasonably think. But what was the big man with the camera saying? And why did he seem so worried?

What Frank was saying, after looking about the room and shaking his head despondently, was, in a low voice to the reporter, "What do *you* think?"

This was the reporter's cue to reply, "Frank, I just don't know. It's certainly a tough one."

"Never went up against anything quite like it."

"What about the other end of the room?"

"Better, maybe, but see for yourself . . ."

"Yeah."

Any Madame Chairman, after overhearing enough of these gloomy exchanges, gained the impression that she had contrived a room to defy the camera, a room photographically unfit. But how had it happened? What was the trouble?

Colby's explanation began with a statement of his own occupational obligations, his duty to the *Transcript*. It would not do for him to turn in a bad picture. Further, he assumed, the Madame Chairman and her committee would not like to appear in one. These suggestions always drew hearty amens from all the ladies, and Colby's austere professionalism seemed to thaw.

The bull's-eye mirror, Colby went on, was a handsome piece, an heirloom worth its pride of place, but did Madame Chairman realize what a reflection from it might do to the picture? The vases, the book ends, all the knickknacks in the bay window—here were fatally distractive details which would cause the "background" to overwhelm the subjects themselves; namely, the charming members of the Committee on Arrangements. Frank was, as I have said, an altogether convincing expositor, and the entire group was soon firmly in his thrall.

After more tense colloquy between Frank and the reporter, Frank would make what was obviously his last-ditch suggestion. It was a desperate remedy, he seemed to feel, but he would ask, anyhow: "Now, if you didn't object to our moving some of this stuff . . .?"

The proposal was so moderate as to bring an immediate sense of relief to Madame Chairman and her committee. Object? Certainly not, and so once again there came into being what was known in the *Transcript* office as the Furniture Moving Act. The ladies themselves, bridling under Frank's sledgehammer compliments, were glad to join in, and if servants were available, they were summoned to help, although the *Transcript's* people usually took on such heavy items as the piano or a big sofa. It is fair to say that we never shirked our own share of the moving. For our private and indefensible ends, the more we moved the better.

The project amounted, roughly, to emptying one half of the room into the other. Anything at all movable or detachable was included in the shift. The ladies were then posed, photographed, rearranged, and photographed some more in that part of the room now so conscientiously protected from undesirable reflections and decorative detail. The finale came when Frank would look at his watch and announce, with an air of dismay, that we were now overdue at our next assignment—to make pictures, so his story went, of the governor or whatever earth-shaking celebrity might be in town—and that having to move so much furniture was why we had fallen so far behind. The ladies were all sympathy, impressed to be sharing our day with such distinguished competition and pleased, too, by the diligence and gravity we had shown in our dealings with them. This was no slapdash performance, and they all knew how perfectly *dreadful* people were made to look in ordinary news photography. As for the furniture, just leave it where it is . . .

The Furniture Moving Act, so far as I could judge, made everybody happy: it flattered the ladies by the extra work so cheerfully carried out in their behalf; its fraudulent quality was entertaining to Colby and the reporter; and the disorder left in its wake was a vengeance, somehow, on the city editor for sending his staff on such worthless assignments.

Frank's other solace, on a bad assignment, was less work than the Furniture Moving Act—indeed, it was hardly work at all— yet it proved equally satisfying to all concerned. It consisted of posing his subjects in various combinations and arrangements, once he had made the single picture he had come for, and then earnestly clacking his shutter at them without any plates in the camera. "I'm afraid the lady moved a little in that one," Frank would say. "I'll have to try it again," and another plateless exposure was solemnly accomplished. A coded announcement by Frank to the reporter always preceded a sequence of dummy shots: "The rest of these are gonna be on the house."

Colby's plateless jocosities once carried us gaily through a long and sweltering July afternoon on the lawn of Craigie House, in Cambridge, where we had been sent to await the arrival of "General Washington," traveling to his headquarters by coach, over the road from Sudbury. Some historical society

145

was sponsoring this bit of pageantry, and a score or more of its members, in colonial costume—the reception committee—were lounging about the terrace when we arrived. The men had laid aside their tricorns and perukes, the women their much larger, and hotter, wigs. All were sweating at a great rate in their finery.

General Washington's livery-stable horses were probably doing their best, but it was soon plain that we were not going to catch the last edition on that day and that we might be waiting some hours for a shot of his actual arrival. So, muttering me his "on the house" line, Frank went bustling among the company, bidding them to get into full costume and to stand by for an important series of photographs. "They want a whole page of this," Frank announced. He looked appraisingly at his subjects, purporting to seek some fine point of dress or personality or physique that would place the individual in one or another of the groups that he was lining up.

For the rest of the afternoon, until he finally made a bona-fide picture of Washington alighting from his coach and we took our leave, Frank kept the whole assembly on the hop, arranging them in big groups, little groups, solos, and frequently reshuffling the combinations. It was necessary each time for me to write down the identifications, and I filled a sheaf of copy paper with the names of our subjects and the colonial officers and dignitaries they were impersonating. Anyone doffing a wig or garment was immediately ordered to get back into full regalia for the next picture. There must have been scores of the plate-less exposures, hot and tiring work, but, like the Furniture Moving Act, something thoroughly enjoyed by everyone.

A typical Colby collision with uniformed authority came one summer morning at the Navy Yard in Charlestown. Colby had made his pictures and set out for the *Transcript*, and I was heading for the gate, on the run, about a half-hour behind him, when a Hearst photographer who was passing called to me. "Better get Colby out," he said. "They've got him locked up in the brig."

I hurried over to the office of the Yard's commander, an urbane four-striper. He accepted, affably, my suggestion that some misunderstanding had occurred, picked up the phone, and listened to a report from the Marine guard. "Well, bring him right over here," he said. Frank, it transpired, had been trespassing in a zone forbidden to civilians, ignoring orders from the guard to halt. He was escorted into the office, plainly in a rage, a few minutes after the commander laid down the phone. An elegantly turned-out sergeant of Marines and two privates, hard-bitten professionals all, were in charge of the prisoner.

"We are sorry to have delayed you, Mr. Colby," said the commander, "and I wish you would tell me just what happened."

"I'm sure I don't know," Frank replied testily. "I was walking along and minding my own business, when *this* boy"— and Frank bent a gaze of contempt at the sergeant—"*this boy* come up and begun hollering at me. Next thing I know . . ."

The commander, seeing that no great gains impended for either side in the dispute, dismissed the guard. We were about to take our own leave when the commander ill-advisedly thought to deliver an appreciation of the Navy's position in the case. "Put yourself in my place, Mr. Colby," he began, soothingly. "Suppose that *I* was a guest in *your* house——"

"Stop!" cried Frank, raising a palm in the manner of a traffic cop bringing everything to a halt. "Stop right there!"

I am sure that neither the commander nor I had the slightest idea of what was coming next. His preamble had seemed reasonable, but Frank was boiling. "I'm not a guest here," Frank went on. He paused dramatically. "I'm a TAXPAYER! I *pay* for this place!"

This was the last argument in the world that the commander

wished to pursue in those low-budget, Depression-ridden days. He began shuffling papers on his desk. I offered thanks and regrets, and all the way back to the office Frank continued to expound his rights and responsibilities as citizen and taxpayer.

Frank's view of the courts and police was unfolded one day in the city room after his son, Warren, had been fined $25 for speeding. Such a penalty, Frank felt, showed a sad lack of judicial understanding. "Now, if I was that judge," he said, "do you know what I would have done? I'd have said to that motor cop, 'Now, you say here that the defendant was doing forty-five miles an hour?'" Frank's tone was silky, as he prepared to trap the miscreant motor cop. "*'How fast was you going to overtake him? Fifty miles an hour, you say? Very well.'*"

At this point Frank seemed to gather judicial robes about himself as he looked first to the hypothetical motor cop and then to the defendant. "'Very well. You, sir'"—to the defendant, who was after all his own son—"' you are discharged —*with honor,*' I'd say. 'And as for you'"—turning to the luckless motor cop—"' Thirty days in jail, you son of a bitch!'"

The *Transcript's* staff included some extremely odd-looking people; their effect on a stranger, especially when two or three of our more outstanding showpieces happened to come within his view at the same time, was numbing. Much as he might wish to take full note of the details, his mind seemed to falter and he was soon doubting his senses. Seasoned public relations men turned tongue-tied and dazed at the sudden appearance of H. H. Fletcher in idle conversation with Mrs. Abraham Lincoln Bowles; they were afraid to look and couldn't bear not to.

Fletcher was the proprietor of the vast religious section of the Saturday *Transcript* called "The Churchman Afield" and "Notes from the Field." Any clergyman could get a story about

148

himself and his church into the *Transcript's* department of religious intelligence simply by sending it in to Fletcher, who would put it into "Notes from the Field." Not unnaturally, there were many who did so: a gratifying growth in Laymen's League membership, a drive for a new carpet for the center aisle, repairs to a steeple, renovating an organ—any of these would find print. "The amount of correspondence involved in the conduct of this department of church news," remarks Joseph Edgar Chamberlin in his book, *The Boston Transcript: A History of Its First Hundred Years* (Houghton Mifflin Company, 1930), "and evoked by it, would be almost incredible to an outsider."

Fletcher had been with the paper more than thirty years, and many believed him a former clergyman, although this was not the fact. He looked much like the bust of Homer which used to be a popular schoolroom decoration, with a white beard and mustache and a rather gloomy cast of countenance. He always wore black, and a ministerial black tie with his white shirt. His general effect was distinctly spectral. But all this might have seemed ordinary had it not been for his habit of inserting, on each side of his head behind the side-pieces of his spectacles, a long envelope. The envelopes projected forward and upward at an angle of some 45 degrees, giving him a rakish and totally unexpected appearance. To look up and see, for the first time, this apparition in its blinders was a unique experience.

Mrs. Bowles was quite old and small, a study in gray: suit, stockings, hair, hat. She walked with the aid of an ebony cane with a silver knob, and her eyeglasses hung by a broad black ribbon. Her hats were Queen Mary peach-basket, and, although she was a kindly person, her expression was that of one about to lose patience altogether with the human race. Through some miracle of survival, a fern and a small rubber plant flourished

149

greenly, despite the steam pipes and grime of the city room, on the top of her ancient roll-top desk.

The typewriter used by Mrs. Bowles must have been the very last of its kind in service anywhere, a machine that antedated the so-called "visible" typewriter and had to be operated on trust, so to speak, by the typist. Its type bars came up from below the roller, striking it on its bottom, quite out of sight. If the typist wished to see how things were going, the whole roller assembly, which was hinged, could be lifted by a handle sufficiently to expose what had been written. One would see Mrs. Bowles serenely pecking away at the keyboard, and at long intervals, as if her curiosity had finally got the best of her, lifting the roller and staring disgustedly, through her pince-nez, at her copy. She seemed to be always expecting to find something better than what was there.

I am not sure, today, whether Mrs. Bowles' department was "Women's Clubs," or "Patriotic and Historical," or both; in any case, she put in a full day at her invisible typewriter. Some of her air of exasperation came, no doubt, from the location of her desk, which stood in the corner of a narrow, slot-shaped room where four or five of the news reporters did their typing and carried on all manner of raffish conversation.

There was on the staff, for instance, a female who managed, unaccountably, to get into almost every paragraph of her writings an example or two of the *double-entendre*. She was a distressingly wholesome creature, beyond the age of mere giddiness, and why so many things that sounded like Freudian slips kept creeping into her prose was a mystery to us all. Yet the most innocent bits of reportage became, in her copy, a Rabelaisian kind of top-shelf literature, and the staff was fond of reading these aloud, with appropriate leering, clearing the throat, and affecting to loosen a too-tight collar at the more significant passages. Readings such as these Mrs. Bowles could appear to ignore on the grounds of simply not hearing them, but the outbursts of H. T. Parker, the *Transcript's* celebrated theater and music critic, were much harder not to notice.

Parker was the most respected, and deservedly so, member of the whole organization: an abrupt, fiery personality, a superior writer and journalist, and among the two or three foremost critics of his day. David McCord's superb little monograph on Parker (*H.T.P.: Portrait of a Critic*, Coward-McCann, Inc., 1937) portrays him better than anyone else could, and I mention Parker here only because his celebrated tantrums, with screams and imprecations, were staged at the very elbow of Mrs. Bowles.

The tantrums were Parker's reaction, as a practicing perfectionist, to what he conceived to be inexcusable failures—that is, any failure—of the office routines affecting his work. On his realizing that an office boy had failed to deliver to him on schedule an edition of the paper, or a cut that he was awaiting, or proofs, or mail, Parker's small, stooped figure would come bounding out of his cubbyhole and land, on perhaps his second bounce, beside Mrs. Bowles. He was like a mechanical toy that jigs or jumps up and down, but the activation in his case was sheer rage.

"Where is that goddam office boy?" Parker would scream. "Where are you, you little cur?"

Parker was never without a cigarette in his mouth; he smoked Richmond Straight Cuts, which were apparently loosely rolled and rather dry, for he gave off ash and sparks as he talked, and in his tantrums he seemed about to burst into flames.

But the noisier Parker became, and the more severe his complaints, the more aloof from her surroundings Mrs. Bowles appeared. Her tempo on her typewriter picked up; she pecked out long passages without lifting the roller for a look at the copy, stopping only to consult, intently, her notes. For her there was no such person as Parker, and I suppose it would be

151

correct to add that, for Parker, in his mood of dissent, Mrs. Bowles had no existence whatever.

Parker used only his initials, H.T.P., in signing his copy; his name was scarcely known outside the world of music and the stage. He lived alone at the Hotel Vendome, where, it was believed by the *Transcript* staff, he had the privilege of foraging in the refrigerators for a late supper around 4:00 or 5:00 A.M., after completing his long-hand critique for that day's editions.

Parker did not live to see the deterioration and ruin of the *Transcript*. He was picked up on the street one winter night in 1934, delirious and in the last stages of pneumonia. There was some unease at the hospital's admissions desk over who would be paying the bill for him. It was inferred from a letter in his pocket that he lived at the Vendome. Further inquiry at the hotel brought a conjecture that the patient had some sort of connection with the *Transcript*, but that was all that the hotel people knew about him. He was not an easy man to get to know.

Whether there ever was in fact such a breed as "our kind of people," given to reading, with satisfaction, the wildly diversified departments produced by the *Transcript's* "editors," I was never sure. But it seems reasonable that for every odd editor, there are equally odd readers attuned to him. In any case, the number of our kind of people, if one applies the term to all the *Transcript's* readers, continued to shrink, and the bundles became even fewer on the circulation delivery trucks, so that by the summer of 1936, at the end of my stay, the circulation stood at a scant 31,000.

●●

CHAPTER ELEVEN

The Transcript:
Virtuosos Without an Audience

THE *Transcript's* quarters, on the corner of Washington and Milk Streets, were part of a weirdly allocated old building in which the paper's "counting room," which could just as well have been tucked away under the roof, occupied the choice ground-floor space. Instead of yielding a handsome rent from some retail establishment, the room was given over to the desks and various clerks and typists in the advertising and circulation departments. Most of the advertising people seemed to prefer their desks to the rigors of finding customers in the world outside, and there was always the chance, of course, that the telephone might ring while they were out. I cannot recall that I ever met anyone from the circulation department during my years there, nor did I ever know the name of any circulation functionary. No one, as I have said, was really interested in circulation. There was a fleet of smart red trucks which the paper chartered to deliver our editions to distribution points, and the owner's name, *Harry Lofchie*, was emblazoned on each, and a brave show they made, backed against the Milk Street curb and waiting for papers. Some were well laden, but the inference that vast numbers of people were standing by throughout Greater Boston, eager for the next edition, weakened every time a sizable truck, complete with driver, would pull out with a solitary bundle of *Transcripts,* bound for heaven knows what one-bundle destination.

In the Washington Street doorway, at the foot of an interminable flight of well-worn stairs, was a large brass sign:

EDITORS TWO FLIGHTS
REPORTERS THREE FLIGHTS

Like many other features of the *Transcript,* the sign was long out of date, since most of the editorial and news staff were on the same floor at the top of the stairs. Halfway up were the sales and fitting rooms of Dunne, the great tailor, where, it was believed by the city staff, the city editor bought his suits at half-price by accepting, with proper alterations, the suit of a customer who had died before it had been completed. In any case, the city editor was the only presentably dressed person in the entire establishment, and the legend persisted that this was why he had been tapped for the job, rather than because of any comprehension of news values.

A partnership of two young lawyers, Lurie & Alper, rented offices just below the city room, and various departments and personalities of the *Transcript* were scattered in closet-like odd spaces throughout the building. I recall looking out a back window on one occasion and seeing a kind of delivery basket traveling from one wing of the building to a window somewhere in Dunne's, and I was informed that this was a transaction between the needle-workers in the rear and the fitting rooms up front. Over everything, especially the windows, lay a heavy deposit of grime, so that one had the impression of a permanent overcast outside.

I doubt that the entire furnishings of the news and editorial areas, including the typewriters, would have brought $250 from any kind of purchaser. The desks, as battered as the swivel chairs that went with them, many of the latter with the back support broken off, were fit for firewood and no more. Most of the desks had a folding top which disappeared when the occupant pressed a button, an action which at the same time caused a typewriter to emerge from a concealed well. The trouble with these was that the locking catch was worn, and when the typewriter was up, a vigorous stroke on the keyboard would cause the typewriter to sink suddenly from view, while the desk top would swing up and out and fetch the unwary typist a smashing blow on the head. There were two or three such desks where no staff man would sit, but visitors who wanted to dash off a note or announcement were always gestured to them with every air of hospitality.

Just off the city room, in the hall beside the elevator, was the toilet which served the news staff and "editors," strictly a one-at-a-time accommodation, filthy and malodorous. Harvard men were relatively few among the staff, but such was the overpowering proximity of the university in the *Transcript's* daily rounds that the toilet was always referred to as "the Harvard Club."

The *Transcript* was celebrating its one hundredth anniversary when I went to work there. Its roster included upward of a hundred persons under the heading "Editors and Reporters," although on examination this category was found to include office boys, telephone operators, and a fair number of individuals entirely unknown to the active news staff. In this latter group was a man who had contributed for several decades an anonymous column of witticisms which appeared weekly—it may have been semi-weekly—on the editorial page. It had a title of its own, "Facts and Fancies," and it was a thoroughly competent piece of work, but it is the simple truth that none of us had ever laid eyes on its author or heard his name; the editor who had taken him on in the first place was long dead and gone, and the "Facts and Fancies" man, who transacted his business with the cashier and never asked for a raise, was as near to a genuine nonentity as an active contributor to a daily metropolitan newspaper could be.

It was against this background of facts that the city room was thunderstruck one day to be handed a Hollywood story that a major studio—MGM, as I recall it—had acquired the script of what most certainly would be an "epic," and that said "epic" script had been written by the "Facts and Fancies" contributor—perhaps I should say "editor"—of *The Boston Evening Transcript*.

Evening-paper news was, in those days, an extremely high-speed affair, and for a time we were afraid that other papers would corral this new local celebrity, our own man after all, before we could. One of our most experienced reporters, Bigelow Thompson, was assigned to hunt him out, and managed, aided by the police listing of Boston residents and a few shrewd conjectures from the counting room, to find him in a lodging house room off Huntington Avenue, where he had apparently spent most of his life. It fascinates me to recall that the "epic" in this case was an account of the house of Rothschild and the family's rise to great power and wealth, and that it was also a smashing success, earning handsomely for its proprietors and adding kudos to its already famous principals. In the hullabaloo the *Transcript's* man seemed to drop even further into obscurity. I have no recollection of his name or of whether he ever repeated his success as a scenarist, but it is my impression that he continued to supply the "Facts and Fancies" column—a man who knew a good thing when he had it.

Any establishment of such great age has its complement of veteran employees, and at the *Transcript* some of them were spectacularly so. There was one aged spinster, an improbable sort in any company, who was pointed out to me as the "editor" of some equally improbable department. I asked how in the world such a woman and such a job had ever got together. The answer was: "Her father used to do it." Changes came hard. It was characteristic of the paper that its column of notes on radio programs was one of the first and the best in print, at a time when other papers were still trying to find a happy formula for ignoring radio or putting it out of business. But for years after the radio receiver had become a self-contained unit in a cabinet, the cut at the head of the *Transcript's* radio column continued to show a set on the order of an early Neutrodyne, all dials and wires, with a towering "loud-speaker" horn of a type that had vanished with the Model T. The devising of a long-needed-two-column head for freaky news stories on page one was regarded as so venturesome, typographically, that the head was named after the editor of the paper, H. T. Claus, who had laid out the specifications for it.

I had only one encounter with the *Transcript's* lawyer, an aged, bearded alarmist who seemed to live even further from the world of reality than some of our own eccentrics. It would have been fatal to any story to allow the *Transcript's* lawyer to read it for possible libel. He would have taken it under advisement for a few days or weeks, unmindful of deadlines or our competitors, and eventually handed it back with a complex warning that it was clearly actionable—as almost any news story is if its subject chooses to sue—and to be published only at intolerable financial risk.

Since his quirks were well known to the news staff, no one ever dreamed of trying out a story on the lawyer. Chance it yourself or throw it away. Whenever I had anything fancy of my own that called for advice, for it would have saddened me to have cost the *Transcript* a libel suit in its days of need, I tried it on Lurie & Alper on the floor below, who enjoyed seeing a tart story in the paper and who helped me just for the fun of it.

The case which brought me into the lawyer's office was pure

157

idiocy all the way. A friend in charge of publicity for the Republican State Committee had given me a campaign song, of the most painful disabilities in all respects, which some local zealot had composed and donated to the committee in behalf of Mr. Hoover. The *Transcript* was, of course, Republican, but this did not deter it from going along with a small bogus story on page one, publishing the verses and conjuring its readers to sing or declaim them at every opportunity.

A day or two after the story appeared, the versifier threatened to sue the *Transcript* for breach of copyright. I was ordered to tell the lawyer the story and reassure him. Our interview began with a stern inquisition into who I was, my past, education, jobs, and such, as if I might be a Trojan horse, foully infiltrated into the *Transcript* ranks by rivals seeking to destroy the sheet. Above all, what could possibly have been my motives in turning in so trashy a jingle? He paid little or no attention to the facts surrounding the story, assuring me that the author could collect thousands from us (nothing more was ever heard from him). We parted in mutual disgust.

The *Transcript's* purchasing agent—although we inclined to think the title was self-bestowed, since no one would have entrusted this individual with such weighty responsibilities as the procurement of newsprint and ink—was a specialist in obtaining trade discounts for the staff, invariably on merchandise in which we had no conceivable interest. A notice that we could buy baseball equipment from Iver Johnson's for the next thirty days at a 10 per cent reduction might appear on the city-room bulletin board, and the purchasing agent, pencil in hand, would come among us inviting orders. His must have been a frustrating life, for nobody ever seemed to need a first baseman's mitt or a pair of shin guards. We'd make the old ones do for another season, we told him. Even more disappointing was the office reaction to his hopeful inquiries about minor supplies such as pencils or copy paper. Etiquette called for morose,

158

even critical responses, and a typical conversation with him was eagerly attended by all within earshot:

"How do you like that new pencil?"

"What new pencil?"

"Why, that new Eagle Mirado No. 174 that you are using."

"I hadn't noticed it."

"Well, don't you think it's better than Eberhard Faber's No. 482?"

"No."

"You don't?"

"I should say not."

"Oh."

The purchasing agent did come into his own each year just before Easter. Through some deal with a wholesale florist, he offered a small discount on lilies, and it was not unusual for a hundred or more orders to come in to him from various departments of the *Transcript*. The pots of lilies were ranged over the floor of the city room to be picked up by their owners, all under the vigilant supervision of the purchasing agent. The lilies engulfed the room, and the story ran that one year the traffic was so heavy and the congestion so demanding that the purchasing agent simply keeled over in a faint, right in the midst of his blossoms.

Even in its leanest years the *Transcript* refused patent-medicine advertising. No great amount of this would have been forthcoming in any case, since the paper held no appeal as a mass market for anything, but nevertheless the blandest cure-all were advised to make their expenditures elsewhere, with one great exception: Cheney's Asparagus Tonic.

Like the "Facts and Fancies" column, the relationship with Cheney's, an ancient drugstore on Union Street just off Dock Square, antedated the *Transcript* staff, and no doubt their fathers as well. Embarrassingly, no literature from Swamp Root, or Beef, Wine & Iron, or Fellows' Compound of Hypophosphites was a whit more exuberant than the claims laid down by Cheney for the wonderful Asparagus Tonic, but the copy never varied from year to year.

Cheney's advertisement appeared each spring, occupying one of the *Transcript's* broad seven-to-a-page columns. Its timing was in the good old spring-cleaning-and-renovation theory, which governed the use of many tonics, and an impressive display of Asparagus Tonic bottles in Cheney's store window coincided with the *Transcript* advertisement. As I recall the advertising copy, it was largely a duplicate of the label on Cheney's bottle: an astonishing list of ills large and small—virtually everything but fractures—which the tonic would alleviate or end altogether. It was indeed a sign of spring, and I think we all enjoyed its recurrence. The tonic is still available at Cheney's, and I dare say many *Transcript* readers continue to swear by it, although the offer on its label has been narrowed somewhat by the passing years and by the skepticism of a despotic bureaucracy in Washington.

The *Transcript* had no rewrite men as such. A reporter who went out on a story either dictated it (with all the punctuation) by telephone or rushed in and wrote it in the office. Everyone was a rewrite man in taking small stories from correspondents in the metropolitan area. On big out-of-town stories, the reporter sometimes had a Morse operator and messenger of his own, and in later years a teletype, and once in a great while the paper sent out two men, to spell each other, on some especially massive trial or hearing where practically verbatim coverage was expected. Ordinarily, one *Transcript* reporter was enough, so it was held, even though he might find himself up against a team of three or four people from each of the other papers. Relations with the other papers were full of warm friendships. Most news and gleanings were shared, for the competitive result of a day's work was not how much exclusive news a man rounded up but how much of it he could get past his city editor and into the paper. The city desks around town were altogether dissimilar: at the *Globe*, dull and cautious; the *Traveler*, a countrified lunge in the direction of *The Front Page*; Hearst, a tough and amiable group of competent professionals.

The *Transcript* city desk was like none of these. On a story of any magnitude or tension it tended to stay out of the line of fire, to leave it all up to the reporter, and to remain more or less incommunicado. On a big two-man story that we were covering for several weeks, a trial, it developed one morning that the principal defense witness had just been arrested on a narcotics charge. We put a bulletin to this effect on the teletype and asked whether anything more was wanted on that circumstance or whether to go ahead with the customary full coverage of the trial. It was about twenty minutes before the session was to open, and we hung eagerly over the teletype awaiting the answer. Just as we were rushing off to the courtroom, the machine stuttered out a reply.

"City desk," so the message went, "wants to know dates you prefer for your vacations."

The same city editor had been, many years earlier, the *Transcript's* bicycle editor, from which post he was elevated to automobile editor as public interest in "the wheel" gave way to the wonders of the motorcar. He continued as automobile editor, more or less emeritus, and one of his perquisites as city editor was the annual junket to the opening of the New York Automobile Show, whence reams of publicity material would be wired to the *Transcript* under his by-line.

Now a pink-cheeked, graying, good-looking man whom everyone liked, the city editor came into the office one morning, Boston bag in hand, bound for New York on the three o'clock train. His was an enormously kindly, friendly personality, quite without the petty qualities of his predecessor, but

161

abrupt, sensational, urgent news was not at all his metier. It disturbed for him what was otherwise a safe and agreeable day's work, full of sociability and all sorts of small diversions. To become caught up in one of those headlong intervals of extemporization that suddenly imposed themselves on a news staff was far from his desire at all times.

On this day all went quietly until 1:55 P.M. (It should be mentioned that the *Transcript* was a ten-minute walk from South Station, and trains for New York left every hour on the hour throughout the day.) At this point the tapper in the city room began sounding a succession of alarms, and our man at police headquarters phoned in to tell us that the new stands at Fenway Park, under construction and almost completed, were on fire and that the flames had spread to two houses across the street. It seemed an excellent break for an evening paper in so solid a baseball town as Boston, but a look of anguish came over the city editor. For a moment he was stunned. Then he pulled himself together, put on his hat and coat in a leisurely way, and picked up his Boston bag. "I must be getting my train," he said cheerily, and left.

There was no assistant city editor or number two to take over, for no one had ever troubled to define such niceties of organization. A characteristically fast and effective job of unorganized activity followed the city editor's exit. "I'll go out," said Karl Schriftgiesser. "Anything is better than sitting around here." An office boy took the city desk phone and assigned the incoming calls for the next hour. Our photographer Frank Colby decided to go along with Schriftgiesser. The make-up man was alerted. Various people started trying to reach the Red Sox business office, the contractor, nearby residents. At around 2:30 Schriftgiesser began dictating his story and Colby came in with some good pictures. Our two-man copy desk shuffled some sort of sequence into the smaller stories, and by three o'clock all was quiet once again, even before the city editor was pulling out of South Station.

The great mass effort of the *Transcript* staff came in the fall, when on each Saturday during the season we produced the Football Extra. This was a genuine *tour de force;* it would have been counted a distinguished piece of work anywhere, and it undoubtedly was the best thing of its kind in print. The *Transcript* was not a hard-drinking place; in fact I recall only two people in the news department who drank, needfully, in the office during the day. But the Football Extra was by way of being a real spree, an afternoon of gaiety, journalism, and alcohol. Best of all, in those Depression days, the Football Extra was a self-financing party for the participants: a man's supply of rum for the afternoon cost about $2 or $2.50, while each of us got $5 for our services. We looked forward to it throughout the week.

The *Transcript's* big Saturday edition, in which almost all its departments were included, closed at 1:15 P.M., and the first item in the afternoon's agenda was the arrival of Billy the Bootlegger, delivering the rum for which he had taken orders the previous day. Billy was a small-time hoodlum, an occasional longshoreman, and he used this latter role to reassure us about the quality of the rum he sold us; the real thing, from Martinique, right off the ship. He wore a cap, blue jeans, and a Navy pea jacket. I blush to realize the extent to which Billy's get-up reinforced his credibility with supposedly well-informed newspapermen, but if his rum was more probably from East Boston than from the West Indies, it was reasonably wholesome and neither crazed nor paralyzed his customers.

Everyone on the paper worked on the Football Extra; we were scattered all over the editorial rooms, wherever a typewriter could be set up. The sports staff was out covering the contests in which we were most interested—that is, the games of about half the Ivy League and four or five Good Schools. The paper had correspondents of its own at twenty or thirty other games and used AP stories for anything else. The end of the Harvard game, which was always covered by the sports editor, closed all the incoming stories, whether they were complete or not, so that the acute work period in the office began around 1:30 and ended, in a prodigious scramble, at about 4:00. In our handling of the copy, a man might be assigned three or four small games or one or two of the larger ones.

The stories reached us in bits and pieces, a hundred words or so at a time, delivered by office boys on the run. Our task was to edit and move along each fragment instantly to prevent any accumulation of arrears with the compositors. This was no great feat during the first half of the afternoon, but as the Harvard game moved into its final quarter and Billy's rum began to assert itself, the pace picked up considerably. By this time we were obliged to have a lead and head in type, representing the latest state of each game, and to replace these as changes in the game warranted. Whenever one of our games ended, we had, also, a final lead and head all ready to send up.

There was much visiting about and sociable drinking during the early part of the afternoon. Tension began with the succession of warnings on playing time remaining in the Harvard game. Our hope was to have our own games complete and with proper heads and leads, and the more information beyond the mere score that could be packed into a lead, the better. Yet nothing could be jumped, and it would have been thought disgraceful to have even a small error in a final score by reason of some hopeful gamble in the closing moments. Almost all the games were played within the same period, but a laggard correspondent might suddenly turn in, after a long silence, a block of copy that called for complete alteration of head, lead, and emphasis, with only a minute or two to do it in. It was, all in all, a stunt, and a good one. We were

164

proud of the result: a solid page one of the best possible football coverage, with any amount more of it inside, and on the street not a quarter-hour after the end of the Harvard game.

Whatever became of the Football Extra edition, once we had seized our own copies and made our way down the long stairs to Washington Street, was a mystery in all the six seasons I worked on it. Copies would not have reached the uptown hotels by 7:00 P.M. Newsboys with big pedestrian corners never seemed to have it. To look for it in the subway was absurd.

The *Transcript's* own newsboy-in-residence was himself a rather mysterious figure. Small, dark, at times seemingly wizened, or at others merely young and skinny, he might have been twenty, or fifteen, or forty. His station was in the recessed doorway of the counting room, where not even the near passerby would notice him. Across the street strong-lunged boys cried the other papers, but there was only one side to Washington Street, so far as the *Transcript* was concerned, and that was our side. I doubt that one could have found another copy of the Football Extra in the entire length of the street.

Our newsboy's voice was never raised. When we passed him on our way home, as he brooded over his unsung and unsold stack of our wonderful Football Extra, we cursed him with all the bitterness of virtuosos deprived of their audience. If only that wretched newsboy would bestir himself. . . .

But he never did.

●●●

CHAPTER TWELVE

The Athens of America

THE BOSTON of the 1930s had two more newspapers than it has today, and the competition in the presentation of the local news was relatively lively. There was little or no solidarity on the part of the press: if one paper unearthed a good story, the others would play it down as far as possible and even ignore it altogether, a tendency which persists today. But the irresistibly big story brought big local coverage, and *The Boston Evening Transcript* was as energetic a competitor as any of the larger papers.

The community, then as now, was fantastically corrupt. Always, in one court or another, some wonderful "case" was unfolding: the Gillette case, the Dolan case, the Coakley case, the Jarvis case, the Rettich case, the Mackey case—cases involving judges on the bench, leaders of the business world, bandits of Alcatraz caliber, and a dependable succession of public officials. I am unable to find offhand the source of Boston's description as the "Athens of America," but America's Athenians of the early '30s included some highly original performers, all operating sometimes under a set of ground rules and local attitudes that would take aback even the most easygoing moralist.

166

There was, for example, the "inspector" employed by the state to make an annual audit of local stockbrokers, one of whom was found to have dissipated some half-million dollars of his customers' money. The inspector, in turn, was found to have been bribed each year for not troubling to "inspect" the actual securities, long vanished, which the broker's balance sheet showed as assets. It was, no doubt, a perfectly commonplace kind of larceny for that period, but the Boston twist was supplied by the inspector's lawyer when I asked him if his client had been fired as a result of the disclosures.

"Of course not," the lawyer replied. "They can't fire him. He's under Civil Service."

A fine fragment of the Boston point of view comes to mind from another bribery case. The chairman of the Boston School Committee, a South Boston dentist, was on trial, charged with soliciting and receiving large sums for job appointments in the schools, and an eminently respectable witness had just testified that he had declined the offer of the position of Director of Music in the schools, subject to a payment of $5,000 to the chairman. Counsel for the defense arose to cross-examine. His technique would scarcely have fooled a child, but it was plain that he fancied himself as embarking on a masterly entrapment of the witness.

"You knew that this job carried a salary of seven thousand dollars?" the lawyer began. Getting an affirmative answer, he shot a meaningful glance at the jury.

"And isn't it a fact that the man who is Director of Music buys *all the musical instruments* used in the schools?"

"I believe that is so."

Another significant glance for the jury, and the lawyer put his next question so casually as to suggest that he hardly dared hope for another affirmative. "And doesn't the Director of Music also buy *all the textbooks and music* used in the schools?"

167

"Yes," replied the witness. "That is my understanding of it."

The cross-examiner nodded sagely. He had got nowhere, but he seemed to feel that the encirclement of the witness was complete. All that remained was to pounce. The pounce:

"And do you stand there and expect this jury to believe that you wouldn't be willing to pay five thousand dollars *for a job like that?*"

Less visible to the community in general than the showier of the "cases" was Boston's status as the national capital, more or less, of the "boiler rooms," that is, rooms equipped with nothing more than a battery of telephones on which salesmen called prospective victims from coast to coast and persuaded them to buy worthless stock. Stock swindlers bobbed up and vanished in other places, but the Boston operators had a perennial quality, and it was no uncommon thing for one of their better coups to yield them a million or two for what amounted to eight or ten months' work.

The secret of the Boston stock swindlers' durability was twofold: they scrupulously avoided swindling any resident of Massachusetts, and federal and state authorities in the Athens of America amiably disclaimed any jurisdiction over what they did from their Boston base to the gullible in other states. I believe there was a tendency for the promoters to tread lightly in other New England states and New York, the farmers of the Middle West and California being the most responsive to the flatteringly expensive long-distance calls all the way from Boston. A single month's telephone bill for one of these promotions ran as high as $125,000, and the telephone company, with its customary efficiency, devised a system of "sequence calls" which enabled a salesman to proceed from one victim to the next with scarcely a moment's delay. He simply provided the long-distance operator each morning with a list of the day's prospects; the calls, beginning in the East and working westward through the time zones as the day wore on, would be dealing with the Californians by late afternoon.

Forecasting a sharp rise in the market price of the worthless stock was the gist of the telephoned sales talk, and a few days later the victim would receive the financial page of a Boston newspaper, proving by published figures of transactions on the Boston Curb Exchange that the rise had indeed occurred as predicted. It was quite easy to make a stock go up and down on the Boston Curb Exchange in those days by means of fictitious trades known as "wash" sales, and after a few weeks or months of correct forecasts over the phone, backed by those reassuring clippings from the newspapers—including *The Boston Evening Transcript*—investors from Ashtabula to Petaluma were ready to get in on the ground floor and stand by for the killing.

"Let the buyer beware" might reasonably have been the motto of the Boston Curb Exchange, which felt strongly in behalf of the constitutional right of one American to swindle another. The Securities Exchange Act of 1934 incurred its immediate disapproval, and the Curb's spokesman, on eventually receiving the first expression of interest in its affairs from the S.E.C., said to me, "It's like living under the dictatorship of a Hitler." But the Curb was not to live long, dictatorship or no: it went hastily out of business the very next day.

Boston's stage censorship seems to generate fewer *causes célèbres* nowadays than it did during the tenure of John M. Casey, a former trap drummer in a burlesque theater who had the misfortune to lose an arm and who became clerk of the city's licensing division and *ex officio* the sole arbiter of what could or could not be said or done on a Boston stage. He was widely hailed for what was called "The Casey System," which few of his admirers ever troubled to explain: it consisted, in brief, of threatening to withdraw the license of any theater, on the grounds of fire hazards or other menaces to the public safety, in which a producer refused to follow Casey's censorial dictates. On occasion, when he regarded a show as too dirty to be tolerable, even with all sorts of deletions and changes— *Strange Interlude*, for example, *The Children's Hour*, and many others—the show was forbidden to open at all. *Juno and the Paycock* was prohibited on the grounds that it portrayed a priest in an unfavorable light. Attempts by producers to circumvent Casey, in various courts, were invariably unsuccessful: the theater owners had no choice but to sit tight and say nothing.

It fell to me to cover in the early '30s a vast banquet which the grateful city tendered Casey on the occasion of his retirement. One phrase in particular stands out from the torrent of city-hall oratory which "paid tribute," as the newspapers like to put it, to the guest of honor, describing him, at the end of his long career, as "a man whose heart is sweet and clean and whose accounts are in perfect order." The climax of the banquet came when the manager of the Old Howard burlesque theater, which had presented without molestation from Casey and with only brief tiffs with the police some of the nastiest shows imaginable throughout Casey's tenure, handed over to him $1,000 in gold as "a token of esteem," etc, etc. Casey's successor, incidentally, was a son-in-law of a brother of Mayor Curley, who said he had no real experience in the theater and no "system" such as Casey's. "I guess I'll just hafta use my head," was his statement to the *Transcript*.

The city censor needed no assists from anyone and held his theater prerogatives strictly for himself, but the New England Watch and Ward Society kept a sharp eye on misdeeds elsewhere, or at any rate, it purported to. Somehow, it never seemed to concern itself with the more substantial criminality of the community, but rather with small moral lapses, a questionable book, an indecent photograph, or the possibility that not all the Mr. and Mrs. John Smiths registered at "overnight cabins"—

precursors of the motel—were in truth man and wife. It was, in short, a livelihood for its executives and one which was easily perpetuated by frightening a sufficient number of donors—usually embittered spinsters—with the proposition that things were rapidly going from bad to worse. I am embarrassed to recall the innocence with which I went to its offices one day, just as a matter of curiosity, to ask why the Society did not move against a massive situation in the police department in which a lieutenant in charge of the Prohibition unit was just about running the city.

I was turned over to one of the Society's principal figures, a man who looked like a caricature of the prurient snoop, with a great air of false piety about him. The phrasing of my initial inquiry was careless and rather vague, and I simply asked why the Society had not taken action against "the big stuff"—hardly the language for a *Transcript* man, a really big situation could mean only one thing: Women. I did not know this at the moment, and it took me some time to realize it.

"You don't understand," he began. "It's not like the old days."

I could not see what the old days had to do with Prohibition, but I nodded. "No, it's different from what it used to be. These women are scattered all over the city. They work by themselves. They have a small apartment, or maybe even a single room, and there's no way of keeping track of them.

"Now, in the old days," he went on, "you simply went around to one of these *places*. Everyone knew where they were. Big places. You simply rang the *bell*——" His voice hoarsened. "They showed you into a *parlor*. A number of young girls would come in. You'd take your *pick*—and you'd *go upstairs with her!*"

The Watch and Ward man seemed to realize suddenly that a highly enthusiastic note had crept into his recital. "So I'm told," he added primly.

There were, of course, other phenomena of the period in the Athens of America that were neither heinous nor detestable. The event known as the Horses' Christmas Tree, for example, was designed to gladden the heart of the Boston work horse, to ply the animal with perhaps unaccustomed delicacies, and to share with it the sense of well-being enjoyed by others at Christmastime.

Handsomely decorated and well supplied with sugar lumps, apples, carrots, and various goodies, the horses' tree was raised each year in Post Office Square, shortly before Christmas, by the Massachusetts S.P.C.A. A great drive was put on to induce the ever-diminishing number of peddlers and draymen still using horses to bring them around to an afternoon of jollification, and no horse went away from the square with the sense of having hung up a stocking that never got filled. The Society's men bustled around from horse to horse, with buckets of water for the thirsty and distributing the gifts. A real old-time horse-drawn traffic jam filled the square.

As a news story, the Horses' Christmas Tree was a punitive assignment, given only to a callow newcomer or to a veteran staff man who the city editor thought needed taking down a peg or two, but it was one of those Boston phenomena involving "our kind of people"—not including, of course, the peddlers and draymen—and it had to be covered. Inevitably, like a college commencement, or the arrival of the department store Santa Claus, or any other annual fixture, the Horses' Christmas Tree had a certain sameness from year to year. To be assigned to it was an indignity, and the news staff, when I first went to work at the *Transcript*, still enjoyed recounting the tale of the reporter who had covered, a few years earlier, the long salvage operations off Provincetown required to raise the submarine *S-4*, sunk with all hands in a collision. It had been a hard and sometimes dangerous interval. The reporter had judged his work to be excellent, and there was a tinge of pomposity in his manner when the story ended and he finally returned to the city room. The city editor, a fire-eater whom I am glad to say I never knew, looked at him coldly. "Down to Post Office Square," said the city editor, "and cover the Horses' Christmas Tree."

As in the case of Sailors' Snug Harbor, on Staten Island, whose supply of indigent old seamen reportedly became so low that it was necessary to ransack the Great Lakes for prospective beneficiaries, the Horses' Christmas Tree was a waning benefaction. Only two horses put in an appearance at its final occasion, shifted by this time to Boston Common, in 1946.

There were other odd assignments, especially when the news was slack and the city editor—the one we disliked—could indulge himself in them. They took us to many a "service club" luncheon, no worse and no better than the same occasions anywhere else in the country: the members sang the same songs—"Jingle Bells," "Smiles," "Moonlight Bay," and such— and there was the same 25-cent fine for the Kiwanian failing to remove his coat on a hot day and lunch in his shirt sleeves. I don't know why I might have expected better, but the food was the same too: fruit cup (canned), cold ham and potato salad in the summer and hot ham and scalloped potatoes in the winter, with a slab of chocolate-vanilla-strawberry ice cream at all seasons to wind it up.

Interviews were another great outlet for the stray thoughts of the city editor, and the *Transcript* always covered at great length the revivalists who appeared every year or two at Tremont Temple, where they usually set up their base camp. I remember one in particular whose posters described him as "The Man Who Looks and Talks Like Abraham Lincoln." He was backstopped by his brother, who sang and played a "genuine gold-plated hand saw." I have heard West Indian café musicians evoke the subtlest and most charming sounds from a

173

hand saw, but the evangelist's brother made it sound like the howl of a coyote or the wailing of the damned. Both men, artfully dressing the part, did have a somewhat Lincolnesque appearance, and neither was at all backward in explaining to the reporters and photographers the points of resemblance. Frank Colby, the *Transcript's* photographer, had no more liking for evangelists than he had for the police, and he had worked out a formula for making pictures of them that was on a par with the great Furniture Moving Act as a matter of self-entertainment. The genial fraud in this case was to insist on a pose showing the evangelist "in action," so to speak, rather than in spiritual meditation or repose or exhibiting his preferred profile, like a Barrymore. The action shot called for raising the right hand, forefinger extended, in a minatory gesture, and cupping the left hand, at about elbow height, as if to receive the coming vigorous downstroke of the right. "And none of that big old smile," Frank would order. "You've got to look serious."

All the evangelists that we ever covered were glad to concur with Frank's suggestions, some of the veterans even striking the prescribed attitude without coaching. In these cases Frank would ask the reporter to correct, slightly, the angle of the left (or right) arm of the subject on the grounds that the hand was too high (or too low). On one occasion we managed to make a picture of two young evangelists of college age—apprentices, one might call them—facing each other in the classic cliché pose, threatening each other with the brandished forefinger.

It was taken for granted that interviews with the evangelists, or the harangues they delivered at their public meetings, would yield nothing substantial in the way of news, and the reporters enjoyed concerting a sequence of behavior that reflected this circumstance and at the same time seemed to befit the occasion. Whether we were taking notes in an interview or sitting at a press table directly in front of and below the speaker at a meeting, the routine was the same: all the reporters would begin writing at top speed with the evangelist's first words. This would continue for two or three minutes. Apparently, every word was being taken down for use *in extenso*, and the evangelist, who had never before found himself talking to so diligent a group of note-takers, was beaming with satisfaction. "Now, the main purpose of my coming to Boston," he would be saying, "is to——" At this point, by prearranged signal, each reporter would stop writing, lean back, and conspicuously return his pencil to his pocket. All would look politely, even hopefully, at the speaker, but the note-taking was plainly over, and the whole group would get up and leave a moment or two later, giving a friendly nod or smile to the speaker as they left. The objective, so amiably realized, was the complete and abrupt melting away, for no reason, of a press activity that had seemed to be going great guns.

●●●

Depression and the Drys

ANYONE who was trying to earn his living through the Depression days is bound to have a hard time recounting the period to a later generation. The same is true of Prohibition, overlapped by the Depression for the final four years of its span. Living under the pressure of these forces in combination, with no end of either in sight, one tended to regard them as a permanent legacy for modern man—conditions which no one esteemed but which nevertheless defied amendment. It was characteristic of President Hoover that, long after Prohibition had become a national disaster, he appointed the so-called Wickersham Commission to make a protracted study of it: Were the Eighteenth Amendment and the Volstead Act functioning happily, or was some slight revision called for? It was characteristic of the commission that it belatedly brought out a vast report which seemed to stimulate more arguments than it settled. The President praised the commission for its selfless devotion to the public interest, the speakeasies renewed their leases, and the Depression dragged on into its fantastic succession of bank failures. *The Boston Evening Transcript* trotted out its biggest type in many a day for the Wickersham findings: "A Wet Commission Makes a Dry Report."

176

The lead on a story from *The Boston Evening American* in 1931, when banks were beginning to fail in dozen lots, preserves for us the usual journalistic spirit of the times, and it would be fair to add that the *Transcript* was willing to report a bank failure as just that and nothing more, without insisting that every closing had a silver lining. The *American's* lead:

"A feeling of optimism pervaded Boston's financial district today, following the first shock of the closing of the 'sound' Federal National Bank, its branches and eight affiliates."

Brokers' market letters of the time showed a similar determination to find the hidden reassurance in the monotonous decline in stocks and the fragility of dividends. A paragraph from a house by the name of Russell, Miller and Company remarked: "New York Central *since it passed its dividend* has shown distinct evidence of important long pull buying. It is likely that Pennsylvania will do the same thing *once its dividend is out of the way* [my italics]. Its price indicates the omission of the dividend." (Note: Pennsylvania did not omit its dividend.)

On the larger view of the general relationship between stock prices and business activity, the Boston firm of Elmer H. Bright and Company issued an opinion that seemed to represent the reasoning of financial experts: "Much has been said about improvement in business being necessary to bring about improvement in security prices. Previously the market has been thought to discount general business improvement. Cause and effect are difficult to diagnose. We believe that rising security prices will give a material impetus to general business."

The principal soothsayer of the period was Roger W. Babson, proprietor of an investment counseling service, who was widely credited—and still is—with having been the unique prophet of the Great Crash in October of 1929. His status is based on a statement in the *New York Times* of September 6, 1929, in which he said, and once again the italics are mine:

177

"*I repeat what I said at this time last year and the year before that sooner or later a crash is coming* which will take the leading stocks and cause a decline of 60 to 80 points in the Dow Jones barometer." Rubbery though this statement was, it caused great indignation in the financial world and among all who were long on stocks, but it caused Babson to be enthroned after the crash as an accredited seer. One is reminded of the tobacco-will-get-you-yet comment made by friends of the heavy smoker who died at age ninety-five.

It was a period when "6% Gold Mortgage Real Estate Bonds" were often found to be mere certificates of indebtedness issued by thoughtful larcenists and worth 5 or 10 cents on the dollar, provided the Securities Holders' Protective Committee had not managed to get there first and lay hold of the last scrapings in the till. A sound ambition for any red-blooded American boy at the time would have been to be a referee in bankruptcy or to organize one of the countless protective committees, or, better still, to become counsel for specialists of this sort. The sheep and the goats were the people with jobs and the jobless, and any sort of job at any wage was better than none. Begging on the streets was less conspicuous in Boston, but in New York one could not walk a block anywhere in the midtown section without being accosted a half-dozen or more times by perfectly proper-looking men and women of all ages— a dime? a nickel? anything? It was impossible to foretell from their appearance which of the others along the sidewalk would prove to be begging. Cancellation of service by telephone subscribers was a regular item of statistical news in the financial pages.

The most corrosive effect of the Depression came from the certainty, from month to month for more than three years, that it was all going to be a lot worse before it got better. Pay cuts announced to be temporary soon proved to be temporary only in the sense that a new and larger cut was in the making.

Prices were, of course, low and continuing to decline. Fifteen or twenty cents would buy a substantial lunch at Woolworth's, where we occasionally invested our quarter-hour at noonday and where many of the customers, after eating a part of the generous portions, would wrap up the remainder in a paper napkin to take home for another meal. It became more agreeable to make a couple of sandwiches at home and lunch on them in the city room, with a 5-cent cup of coffee from Sadie Kelly's Spa, downstairs on the Milk Street side of the *Transcript's* building, brought by the office boy. This led to much expertise among the staff on how to make a proper sandwich—that is, one that would neither dry out nor become soggy—and it was found that large leaves of lettuce effectively insulated the sandwich filler, for both purposes.

More intricate were the techniques of applying the wonderful new do-it-yourself half-soles which the dime stores introduced along toward the bottom of the Depression. I am sure there were more *Transcript* shoes with holes in the soles than without them; if a man wore his rubbers throughout the day in the city room, it was not necessarily on account of the weather but rather the condition of his shoes.

The dime-store half-soles, like the shoes for the Turkish Army, came in three sizes only: large, medium, and small. They were thick rubber slabs, heavily corrugated, and they gave the wearer the impression that he was walking about on something like snow tires. A pair of the soles came affixed to a cardboard instruction sheet, with a small metal grater and a tube of powerful and extraordinarily quick-acting cement. The soles themselves were impregnated with some equally abrupt adhesive, protected by a rubbery sheet which was to be stripped off at the very last instant before slapping the new sole onto the old. One began by roughening the soles with the grater

179

and spreading on the cement from the tube. Before this could dry, the new sole had to be in place—the point of no return—and the final stage consisted in whacking the shoe violently on the floor to make sure that everything was stuck fast. Any surplus projecting around the edges was simply to be trimmed off with a knife, so the instructions read.

The soles must have been made for an extremely wide-footed trade, for the surplus was extensive. The rubber was tough—the uppers of a pair of cheap shoes thus renewed would go to pieces before the rubber showed wear—and it was hard for a man to slice around the edges without achieving the effect of a gadrooned border or a series of angular slashes, which led to much airy comment in the *Transcript's* city room.

A reporter would appear of a morning affecting an elaborately formal manner, sit down at his desk, and begin, foppishly, buffing his nails on his coat sleeve, stopping from time to time to look at them complacently. This could mean various things: that he had just had some preposterous adventure on an assignment and was willing to talk about it if pressed, or that he was wearing some new purchase from Filene's Automatic Bargain Basement, or that he just resoled his shoes with the new dime-store materials. In the last case he would cross a leg so as to show, conspicuously, his handiwork. Comments were immediate.

"He certainly missed his cast on that right shoe."

"I like that sawtooth edging."

Shortly before the do-it-yourself half-soles came in, I was eking out a few extra weeks of use from my solitary pair of shoes, which had holes right on through the inner sole, simply by wearing my rubbers indoors and out. A sardonic friend from Omaha happened in at the *Transcript* office and remarked that, although the weather was fine, I had prudently worn my rubbers. "This is the Boston act, I suppose," he said. "A real Bostonian, eh?" I told him with some hauteur that I preferred the rubbers to walking on no soles at all, and I duly confounded him by taking off a rubber and showing him the hole. Most of us got our shoes at a chain of one-price shops whose shoes at that time cost $3.20. They looked quite all right when new, but they stretched and bulged into odd shapes, and the soles simply could not take the running around that we gave them. The shoes, combined with a dollar shirt from Raymond's, a ten-dollar suit from Filene's Basement, a tired necktie, and a ruinous hat were the uniform of the day—an inexpensive outfit and looking every nickel of it.

The instantaneous view of the Depression in action—or, rather, as an interval of suspended human activity—was afforded by the Times Square breadline, in New York. Its focal point was no more than a counter, in the northernmost part of the Square, around 45th Street, as I recall it, at which a cup of coffee and two doughnuts were handed out gratis to all comers. This particular breadline—and there were many others scattered around the city—was a benefaction from William Randolph Hearst, and its peak of activity was timed to confront the evening theatergoers with a reminder that many of their fellow citizens were having a rough time of it.

Distribution began somewhere around 7:00 or 7:30 P.M., I believe, but the line would begin to take form as early as six o'clock. By 7:00, there were thousands of men, two abreast, in the line, which had doubled back and forth in long serpentine folds, each perhaps a block long. While the line waited for handouts to begin, it was of course stationary, and there was the spectacle: thousands of able-bodied Americans, young and old, waiting quietly for their handout. To see the line for the first time, as I happened to, in a January blizzard was to wonder what on earth it could be. The realization was slow, hardly credible, that this pattern of dark shapes was made up of men, ordinary men, who were hungry enough to stand there

181

in the storm, in the glow of the marvelously irrelevant electric advertising displays, the finest of their kind in all the world.

I have read little or nothing about the Times Square bread-line in the years that followed, although it has seemed to me ever since one of the great touchstones of the Depression years. Somewhere in the literature of the Depression, it ought to claim a few pages, as indeed should the neatly dressed men, each with his crate of apples, selling them on the street corners at a nickel apiece. Where did they get the capital to buy a crate of apples, and why apples instead of lead pencils or shoelaces?

The begging, unabashed, was everywhere, and I am reminded of a conversation overheard in a small hotel where I spent a few days in the forepart of 1932. The hotel was in the West 40s, just east of Broadway, relatively new, well furnished, and I was staying there because in this convenient midtown location a room and bath were to be had for $10.50 a week. But its clientele, embarrassingly at times, was goons and hoodlums, looking like fiction characters, minor employees of the gambling and bootlegging factions, hired to protect deliveries and collections at a fairly low level. The general tone of the hotel and of the whole Depression-ridden neighborhood is in an anecdote which an especially formidable-looking hoodlum was telling two of his cronies as we all stood waiting one evening for an elevator in the lobby.

"Here was this old guy," said the hoodlum, "not a bad-looking old guy, but I seen he was gonna put the bite on me. So just as he comes up to me I says to him, 'Hey, Buddy,' I says, 'could you let me have a dime for a cup of cawfee?' Jeez, y'outa seen his face. I thought I'd die laughing."

Most of the good restaurants along Park Avenue were posting their menus outside to attract passersby, and the *prix-fixe* $1 dinner was a standard offering up and down the street in places where $1 today would fall short of paying for a cock-

182

tail. The usual breakfast price in cafeterias and drugstores was 20 cents for orange juice, bacon and a fried egg, toast, and coffee. The hitch was that too many people could not afford these prices, or any prices at all.

Somewhat less realistic was the direct-relief scheme proclaimed by Aimee Semple McPherson, who came to Boston in one of the bottom periods of the Depression on an evangelistic crusade. The reigning local queen of the headlines at the time was a young widow who who had just been acquitted of the murder of her husband. Her trial lasted for weeks, and no aspect of her life and personality was too trivial for press attention. Of her housewifely qualities one sob sister wrote, admiringly: "She keeps a very neat cell." She was, without doubt, at the time of Aimee's arrival, the most widely known woman in Massachusetts, and it was inevitable that they should team up.

First on their agenda was an evening meeting in the Boston Arena at which the young widow would be immersed by Aimee in a tank of water and "saved." This occasion drew an overflow crowd, indicating plainly that the young widow could be useful in other capacities, and it was announced that she would take charge of a great new welfare program—co-director with Aimee was, I believe, her title—for distributing food parcels to the needy.

The immersion in the tank had been a morning-paper story and consequently not covered by the *Transcript*. But as the *Transcript's* man responsible for news of Aimee from 9:00 to 2:45, it fell to me to cover the first distribution of the parcels. An unoccupied basement near Copley Square was the headquarters, but when Frank Colby and I arrived at the appointed hour, the young widow was the only person there, and the total largess for the needy consisted of two cardboard cartons, each containing about $3 worth of canned goods and staple foodstuffs. The cartons, she explained, were of course only

183

samples; more would be forthcoming. But after Colby made a picture and we left, we heard no more about the young widow and the direct-relief program, and whatever became of the two cartons of groceries we never learned. The deal with Aimee had cooled suddenly.

I must say that during the week, more or less, in which I followed her activities, never once did Aimee fail to maintain her faultless façade of affability, graciousness to any and all of the press, and impenetrable aloofness from embarrassing questions. The same was not quite true of her entourage, one of whom was a comic figure of heroic dimensions, a bulky and unbelievably stupid young man whose name I have forgotten and who was always addressed as "Brother" by Sister Aimee and her staff.

On the first morning of the assignment I arrived at nine o'clock at the large parlor of Aimee's suite in a second-rate hotel. Her secretary, an extremely good-looking girl, invited me to wait until Sister was ready for visitors, and I was sitting there reading a paper when Brother came in.

"G'morning," he said to the secretary and unhesitatingly set a course for the door of what was obviously Sister's bedroom.

The secretary, more sensitive than Brother to what his actions might imply to a third party, called out to him sharply. "Brother, Brother," she said, "Sister *isn't up yet.*"

Brother came to a halt, but it was plain that the secretary's statement was causing no more than a "so what?" reaction in his thinking. The secretary was taking no chances that Brother would be able to add up the situation correctly without assistance. "Come and meet this reporter from the *Transcript*," said the secretary. Her tone was so firm that even Brother suddenly got the idea. I think he had failed altogether to notice my presence up to that point. He came over to me, beaming. "Pleased to meetcha," said Brother, and sat down beside me.

We conversed idly about Brother's adventures on tour, and

we kept getting back to his main preoccupation, that his feet were giving him trouble. He was so talkative that I was curious about what he might say of the man who had been so egregiously identified with Aimee's affairs at the time of her famous "kidnaping" a decade or so earlier. Brother's face darkened at the question.

"I'm a man of God," Brother declared, although this was hardly the first impression a stranger gained of him, "and I don't believe in vi'lence. But when I think of what this little woman had to go through on account of him, I'd just like to get my hands on that son of a bitch!"

Some companies expanded their business and profits right on through the Depression, but I doubt that any of us at the *Transcript* were aware of them. We were all so involved in the paper and so dependent on it that prosperity elsewhere, while the *Transcript* was faring so poorly, was inconceivable. I believe, on the basis of figures shown to me many years later, that the paper's losses were overstated to us, but its circulation and advertising were certainly shrinking from month to month.

The darkest news for us came every year or so with the announcement that all hands would meet in the city room at 3:15 to hear a report from the president of the company, George S. Mandell. We all liked him, a kindly, remote personality, an improbable executive for any sort of enterprise, let alone an evening paper. He was a devoted fox hunter and horseman, with a limp and a stoop from many tumbles, and his small cluttered office usually contained several bits of tack that he had brought into town for repair. My chief visual memory of him is of his limping through the city room, swinging a bridle or stirrup leather, humming to himself, and bowing and smiling to anyone who caught his eye. I doubt that he knew the names of half the staff.

Turnouts for these meetings included only the news and editorial people and those who worked in the "counting room."

The employees under various union contracts had no reason
to attend, for they were not paying union dues for the purpose
of negotiating wage cuts for themselves. I never heard of any
wage cut being accepted by the typographical unions throughout the Depression and the final years of the *Transcript.*
(When I left the paper in 1936, the printers were said to be
paid $57.50 a week, while Henry Claus, the editor and a really
superior person, was down to $50 a week.)

The meetings were brief, merely a formal ratification of
rumors that had preceded them for weeks. The extreme rumor
was, of course, that the *Transcript* would suspend publication,
and I think we always felt bucked up, if not downright cheer-
ful, when the Old Man would begin his statement with word
that this was not so: the *Transcript* was not suspending publication. But it was true, he continued, that losses were mounting, and it was his sad duty to inform us that, effective
immediately, all salaries would be reduced by, etcetera, etcetera.
It was simply then a case of going home and breaking the
news to the family: if things had been bad, they would now
be worse. I think we felt as sorry for the Old Man, for being
obliged to make such embarrassing announcements, as we did
for ourselves.

In certain other respects the Depression was more entertaining, especially in the great numbers of important personages
whom it was constantly whittling down to boy's size. No sooner
did one of these magnificoes perceive that the economy had
"turned the corner," as the favored cliché of the time put it,
than a new flurry of failures, foreclosures, and utterly novel
disasters would break out.

The reassuring speeches of President Hoover always seemed
to presage some altogether new setback. My friend E. B. Sar-
gent, whose desk adjoined mine in the city room, shared with
me a joint stock account—small but absurdly active—and we

picked up a point or so on many occasions by going short on odd lots whenever a presidential speech or message was imminent. The cyclical theorists, chart readers, economists, and rabbit's-foot touchers never had such infallible short-term guidance as was theirs for the simple act of coppering the sanguine utterances of President Hoover. And like Prohibition and the Depression itself, there were times when it seemed as if he would be with us forever. His speeches seemed to me dull and much too long, impaired also by the muttering monotone in which he read them and his occasional struggles with the odd word he seemed to be encountering for the first time. "Auspices" was one which tormented him especially, and I often wondered why he allowed in his text words that repeatedly trapped and tripped him.

The great argument after a major speech by Mr. Hoover was not over whether one agreed or disagreed with it, but rather over what on earth the speech had meant. It was hard to call his position mistaken, for somewhere among his musings might lie quite an opposite possibility. I have always counted the following lines, on the likelihood of there being a second world war, as one of his more sibylline obfuscations:

"Certain types of propaganda are today fertilizing our soil for our entry into war. For instance, we are assured that a great war in Europe has made a general war inevitable every hundred years since the Romans kept the peace. And until mankind makes much greater progress it will continue to be inevitable. But the pounding in of that phrase is either sensational journalistic speculation or European propaganda. Furthermore, it is dinned in our ears that we shall inevitably be drawn into this inevitable war. That depends upon our own will to keep out." Corn, at Iowa loading points, was fetching some 6 or 7 cents a bushel, and the well-to-do, of whom a few still remained, were hoarding canned goods against the threats of Milo Reno and his proposed "farmers' holiday."

187

The real fun figures of the time were, of course, the bankers and financial experts. I had found in my teens that my bank would no more lend me money for playing the market than it would underwrite a system for shooting dice or betting on horses according to their post positions. It had astonished me, therefore, on settling down in Massachusetts at around the peak of the boom in the fall of 1928, to hear my new friends tell how their banks had helped them to buy the rather large blocks of Electric Bond and Share, Radio Corporation, Penn-road, and other favored securities that they were holding. The banks were, in fact, no wiser than Joe Doakes. The 1929 crash in itself plunged many of them into insolvency, not because of a run by depositors who wanted to get their money out, but because the bank examiners found they had made loans so hopefully that they could no longer meet their obligations.

One of the financial remedies attempted by the Hoover Administration was a ruling by the Comptroller of the Currency, whose name I recall as John W. Pole, that banks would be permitted to carry bonds in their portfolios at par, without regard to the market price, which was often anywhere from a half to a tenth of that figure. This remarkable concept received little or no comment at the time, and I have never heard it mentioned in the years that followed, but it still sounds to me like something out of Lewis Carroll. True, the resulting balance sheet might appease the examiners, but what was to happen to this delightful mark-up when the bank needed some fresh cash and tried to sell these same bonds?

The investment trusts proved to have little more trading acumen than the man in the street, and many of them managed to trade themselves into extra losses during the long slide. Their method was simple: sell out at the bottom of a sharp decline; take courage at the next temporary rise and buy in at its top; repeat the performance as long as the capital lasts. Statisticians have estimated that many investment trusts would have been more successful had they invested at the peak of the boom in every company listed on the New York Stock Exchange and then simply sat tight on their holdings for the next ten or twenty or thirty years. Much the same illness seemed to afflict the mutual funds in the sell-off of 1962, when the shrinkage of assets in all but a few funds proved to exceed the decline in the Dow-Jones averages.

A few cool heads must have made great fortunes in the Depression. I have in mind a Boston patriarch who converted all his securities into some millions in cash in 1928 and reinvested just before the bank holiday in 1933. His son explained the father's reasoning to me as follows: "If the country is going to hell, it won't make any difference anyhow, but either the country *is* going to hell or else General Motors is dirt cheap at fourteen dollars a share." A whole building full of finance committees and statistical wizards could have worked long and hard without reaching an equally profitable conclusion.

Boston was never quite able to make up its mind about Prohibition. Through the final years of it the city was under the thumb of a police lieutenant who made no bones about being the man in charge. His connections among the higher-ups were widely conjectured, but nothing of that sort ever came to light. He raided or not, as he saw fit, and that was that. The result was that drinking and bootlegging were tolerated in Boston, provided the surroundings were unattractive. To buy a visitor a drink of whisky in the bar frequented by newspapermen, one escorted him to a rather dirty basement kitchen where, surrounded by garbage cans and the splatter of dishwashing, the proprietor filled a tiny shot glass for the *bon vivant* from a pint bottle labeled Golden Wedding. Take it or leave it.

New York, by contrast, had speakeasies in abundance for every taste and purse. The dollar volume in sales and in protection money must have been astronomical, for these were well-stocked, heavily patronized places that prided themselves on supplying almost any drink called for.

I tried once, on returning from the wonders of New York, to expound the virtues of more variety in his bar inventory to the charming old Irishman who offered the supposed Golden Wedding and only one other item, needled beer. He had just set before me a small glass of needled beer, and I had laid my half-dollar for it on the bar. He listened indulgently to my preachment. He looked at the small glass of beer, then at the half-dollar, then at me, and said with a winning smile, "*This* is all right."

Of all the comic figures generated by the Depression and Prohibition, I recall Professor Irving Fisher of Yale as unique in his misconception of both issues. There were, of course, millions of others who had miscalculated the stock market and who were sure that Prohibition was a blessing, however much disguised, but few were so prominent and so excessively verbal as this revered economist. On financial subjects he managed to give the impression that it was the market that had made the mistake rather than himself, and he continued to make countless speeches on economic affairs long after another man in his position might have seriously considered taking up some new line of work. He was a rabid Prohibitionist, and during the year that I worked on *The Boston Herald*, before shifting to the *Transcript*, I covered a big Symphony Hall meeting of drys who turned out to get the straight of it all from the learned professor. I reported him at length in the *Herald*, but no one seemed to take his figures amiss, with the result that I sent a letter about them to the editor of *Commonweal*, which was very nearly the only respectable anti-Prohibition weekly of that time. The letter, published in its issue of November 6, 1929, was as follows:

"In your issue of October 16 there is a reference to Professor

Irving Fisher of Yale upon which I should like to elaborate somewhat.

"On October 13 Professor Fisher spoke on Prohibition here in Boston, and if my ears heard him correctly, he offered the following mathematical absurdity: a) that drinking today is some 15 percent in extent of pre-Prohibition drinking; b) that from 1920, the advent of Prohibition, the dry move showed a steady gain until 1925; c) that from 1925 to date, one half of this gain was lost.

"May I suggest that a graphical representation of this hypothesis would show that, taking pre-Prohibition consumption as a basis of 100, Professor Fisher's graph would have to drop to minus 70 in order to 'lose half of its gain,' and wind up at plus 15?

"Just what degree of drinking is represented by minus 70?"

In the lean summers of the Depression, I used to spend a week or ten days of my vacation with the Coast Guard on one of its regular patrols. A reporter who could write an ordinarily interesting account of a patrol was always welcomed by the service as a wardroom guest, and the only cost to him was his mess bill, which ranged anywhere from $5 to $10 a week. Why more newspapermen did not avail themselves of these pleasures I have never understood, for it was like having an ocean-going yacht at your disposal along the coast of northern New England. Every patrol yielded its magnificent seafaring scenes and some bizarre adventure, and Prohibition often intruded in all its absurdity.

One summer a year or two before Repeal, I was enjoying a cruise on the spacious old cutter *Mojave*. We anchored off a small air station that the Coast Guard had recently set up at Salem Willows, and the officers were whiling away the day by taking rides, hospitably offered by the station's commander, in a new amphibious plane. Suddenly came radio instructions to locate and shadow the rumrunner *Pronto,* then at sea some thirty-five miles east of Gloucester and seeking to make a shore contact that night with a speedboat from the Cape Ann area. So ran the message from Intelligence.

The people in a Navy or Coast Guard vessel always count that day lost when the ship's movie is not shown, and an hour or so after clearing Salem the captain decreed it time for the show. Evening, the usual time, might find us otherwise engaged, he felt, and he was quite right.

I came on deck at the end of the movie, just after sunset. The afterglow was fading, and the sea and clouds were a pearly gray, an opalescent effect. The *Mojave's* engines were stopped. I realized suddenly that I was looking at our quarry, the *Pronto,* lying motionless in the twilight calm, hardly 100 yards away: a 110-foot converted subchaser from World War I, powered by twin-screw diesels. Her home port was Bridgetown, capital of Barbados, and she was so deeply laden with her cargo of Belgian alcohol that she looked, with scarcely any freeboard, almost like a small submarine. Two salty-looking characters in rubber boots and black oilskins were lounging outside her wheelhouse, and even as I stood gaping at the first genuine rummy I had seen in operation, they disappeared inside, and almost immediately *Pronto* made off toward the west.

The prodigious game of tag that followed, carried on at a speed of about twelve knots, could not have been more exciting at ten times that speed. *Mojave's* maximum was around thirteen knots, about two more than *Pronto* seemed to have, but the rummy's short turning radius, with her twin screws, kept the contest even, and she could be off on a new course by the time we were just beginning to swing around in pursuit. It was easy to keep *Pronto* in sight in the twilight, but if she once got beyond the reach of our searchlights in the dark, we should probably lose her. The cutter had no right to interfere with a vessel of foreign registry on the high seas, so that all *Mojave* could do was watch the rummy in hope of capturing the speedboat that was seeking to take part of her cargo ashore, and, at any rate, of preventing their contact.

The situation was exasperating to *Mojave's* captain. After several especially quick changes of course, just before dark, he ordered a seaman armed with a machine gun to report to the bridge. A round-faced youngster responded, looking much too young to be lugging so threatening a weapon. "Get down there on the port rail and stand by," the captain ordered. "Don't fire until I give the order." But then, as the boy was scuttling away with his gun, still within hearing, the captain shouted, somewhat ambiguously it seemed to me, "I'll fill the bastard full of lead!"

I was enchanted, waiting for what might happen next. Out of such stuff are international incidents made. Both vessels were on a straight course, *Mojave* about 100 yards astern of *Pronto* and coming up on her with our two-knot advantage of speed. *Mojave's* cutwater was headed directly for the exact center of *Pronto's* stern, and *Pronto* seemed to be slowing. With a collision only a few feet away, *Mojave* turned ever so slightly and swept past the rummy. At the same time there was a great thumping, smashing of glass, shouts, and angry words.

My first thought was that the lad with the machine gun must have cut loose on his own, and I hurried out to the wing of the bridge to look. Our bow wave was just rolling across *Pronto's* deck, and the two salty characters in oilskins were knee-deep in water as they ran to close a hatch on the bow. The thumping sounds were continuing and proved to be a barrage of potatoes, from the large, ventilated lockers on deck where we stored our vegetables, which two or three dozen of *Mojave's* people were heaving at *Pronto's* wheelhouse.

Pronto dodged and twisted, barely within the reach of our searchlights, until around midnight, when she laid a course for the tip of Nova Scotia, her shore arrangements a failure for

193

the time being. As she settled on her new course, a jaunty blinker message in Morse came from her: "Thanks for the spuds. Look out for the rocks. Good night."

Potatoes, I learned, were the usual missiles in harassment of the rumrunners. Another favored tactic was for a cutter to lie alongside to windward of a rummy, as near as possible, and blow her boiler tubes, giving the rummy a thick coating of soot. But *Pronto's* time was running out. About a week after I had returned to Boston, a short paragraph with a New London dateline brought word that *Pronto* had been rammed and sunk the night before off the Connecticut coast by U.S.C.G. cutter *Argo,* and what became of the two salty characters in black oilskins, I never did learn.

When legal liquor returned with Repeal in 1933, Boston was no better prepared for the occasion than it had been for Prohibition. It was a festive evening, the crowds were enormous and the drinks in general not very attractive. The Scollay Square neighborhood served whatever was called for—scotch, rye, bourbon, brandy—but in many places it all came out of the same bottle. Jake Wirth's, the old-time German restaurant, was celebrated for its varieties of draught beer in pre-Prohibition days, but the fine Latin motto carved above its bar mirror, "*Suum Cuique,*" had been only a mockery during the long near-beer interval. Now, jammed to capacity with ecstatic beer drinkers, Wirth's was coming into its own again.

On a roundup of the evening for the *Transcript,* I dropped in at Wirth's to get a few pointers on beer. Wirth's head waiter, who worked for the restaurant for sixty-five years, was known to the world as "Pop," a slender little man who always wore a black draught cap and whose manner with customers, in contrast with that of German waiters in general, was always charmingly urbane. I found him at the fringe of the crush around the bar, watching reflectively the customers, who were

194

acting as if this were the last chance at a seidel of beer they would ever have in their lives.

Pop was embarrassed when I asked him about the beer, but he was too fastidious a host and too conscientious a restaurateur to lie about it. Regrettably, he said, Mr. Wirth had been so late in applying for the new liquor license that it had not yet been granted.

"You mean—" I began, with a nod toward the merrymakers at the bar.

"Right," said Pop. "Near beer. Still near beer, the same as yesterday."

PART THREE

●●

CHAPTER FOURTEEN

Dream of Glory:
The New Yorker

AN ADVENTURE with Harold Ross and *The New Yorker* interrupted for me the gloomiest effects of the Depression in the winter of 1931–1932. The prestige of Ross's magazine, especially among newspapermen, was incalculable at the time: business was still declining; jobs at any old wage were impossible to get, once a man became unemployed; but *The New Yorker* was growing rich, as successful financially as it was in the wonderful new journalism that Ross had conceived for it.

I made few attempts—none that I can recall—to write for magazines in my first year with the *Transcript*, largely, I suspect, because I had a horror of rejection and I did not wish to add that possibility to the other aspects of a Depression day. My excuse at the time was the urgency of my work as a news reporter: much as I needed the extra money, I had to conserve my energies for the *Transcript*, although it was quite true that one of the great pleasures of an evening-paper job was the complete breakoff, occupationally, at the end of an afternoon with the certainty that I need not give a thought to work until the next morning. I picked up an occasional $10 for a column on some light subject for the editorial page, and this, I told myself, was bound to enlarge my reputation, even though the fee would do little more than provide a week's groceries. At Depression prices in 1930 and 1931, when we doubled up in our too-big house with a Navy officer and his family, for a household of ten, our outlay for meat, fruit, and vegetables, bought quite without stint but only after the fiercest haggling at the open-air market in Dock Square, was around $12 a week.

Reviewing books for the *Transcript's* big Saturday edition was purely honorific; the stipend was the book and that was all. In my latter years there I acquired a minor treasure trove in the mystery stories that I reviewed for a department called "Rogues' Gallery," named, I believe, by C. B. Palmer, who was editing the Saturday magazine and who went on to greater things at the *New York Times*. The mysteries were great sport to review; anywhere from ten to twenty came in each week, and I unloaded them all, at 50 cents a copy, on a suburban bookseller who agreed with some reluctance to buy all that I brought him, without regard to quality. He was torn between the low price and the risk of being left with unsold copies of the poorer stories, for those were the brave days when publishers would not reimburse a bookseller for the return of any books that remained unsold, and the bookseller was that much more alert to the content of what he bought for his inventory. His failures went, not back to the publisher, but to a bargain table of his own, and my man came near balking at some of the shoddier specimens I provided. A few publishers were so mean-spirited as to rubber-stamp on the flyleaf "Review Copy," in the hope of preventing a resale; others pasted on the inside front cover, for the same purpose, instead of simply folding it in, a slip containing information about the publication date and price. A reviewer dealt with such tactics by omitting to review the book and by lending it around among his friends. If times were tough for publishers, they were even tougher for the reviewer.

Dream of Glory: The New Yorker

Extra money of any sort was scarce when David McCord suggested to me one day in 1931 that I ought to try out a light piece on *The New Yorker*. His own prose—witty, elegant, and original—found a ready market there. For me it was a heady idea, not only to be in print in such company but also to take in one of the supposedly big fees that Ross was paying, but I was sure the magazine was far beyond my capacities. McCord persisted in his encouragement: he would write Katharine White, who was Ross's editorial factotum; he would read the piece, if I wished, before I submitted it.

Still in its early years, *The New Yorker* was the most attractive vehicle in the world for a writer of comedy or light criticism. The risk for me, as I saw it—and, in retrospect, I believe correctly—was in sending down a dud or two, by way of beginning, and thus identifying myself, a writer of no status whatever, as a nuisance. Despite the need of money, I waited until a subject came to hand which seemed just about writer-proof; I wrote the article and with McCord's blessing sent it to Mrs. White.

I have forgotten the amount of the check which came with such marvelously unexpected promptness almost by return mail, with a pleasant note from Mrs. White. The fee was somewhere around $70 or $80, as I recall it, and I believe there were even some odd cents in addition, for these were the days when Ross was trying to be extremely businesslike—paying according to length, and no sloppy rounding off to the nearest fiver. But it was about two weeks' *Transcript* pay for some four hours of work divided between two evenings, and therein lies the tantalizing, plaguing, frustrating aspect of writing for a market: if that's all the time it takes and the fees are so good, why not do it more regularly? Ross once paid me $500 for a piece, occupying a single magazine page, which I wrote in a short afternoon, but it was years before I had another subject that seemed right for his particular wants.

201

It Has Its Charms ...

Anyone working for fees or commissions who is not a smashing success can have trouble in explaining this sort of predicament to his family and friends—perhaps even to himself—and all the more so when money is painfully scarce. The tendency is to reason that at the rate of $100 or so for an afternoon or evening of work, the writer has merely to apply himself in order to take in $30,000 or $40,000 a year, allowing of course for a day off every now and then, and if A won't buy it, try it on B.

My own failing was partly timidity and partly a genuine inability to enlarge my production, fees or no fees. The year 1931 brought me three more successes with *The New Yorker*—four offerings in all and four acceptances; but however welcome the money and the satisfaction of writing for Ross, I could not conjure up additional subjects for him.

So the score stood toward the end of the year, when it occurred to me to try out a parody of a feature which appeared from time to time in the "Talk of the Town" section of miscellaneous odds and ends, written by the staff and carrying at its end a composite signature, "The New Yorkers." The recurring item that offended me was one of those ever so folksy little rambles in an obscure neighborhood of Manhattan, where the writer was always coming upon some quaint old business sign, which led to the discovery of an old family, or an old partnership, or perhaps just an old man, who had been engaged for god-knows-how-many years as a master in the craft of making meerschaum pipes, or riding crops, or bass viols, or footstools. Sometimes the subjects unearthed on these rambles were processors, like shad boners or binding restorers, but more often they were the patient, skilled, devoted, old-style makers of the finest hand-crafted whatever-it-was money could buy.

My parody was simply based on the all too reasonable proposition that one of these shops was much the same as the next, differing only in the names of the principals and its lo-

202

cation and in the nature of its great specialty. This being the case, the parody was written with blank spaces for these items, to be suitably filled in. The heading for it was a long blank, followed by a plural *s*. It concluded, as *The New Yorker* pieces seemed to do, with the names of celebrities who patronized the quaint old place. Lady Mendl was one, and General Pershing was another (he had one of the ——s with him in France). The last line of the piece I recall with some self-complacency: "The most expensive —— they ever made was purple and gold, inlaid with ivory. It was for Battling Siki."

A writer's view of his own work is not necessarily trustworthy. I found a copy of the blanks piece a few years ago and reread it with enjoyment, as much, in fact, as I ever gained from a piece of my own. Yet I remember dissuading James Thurber, when he was sending the *Atlantic* chapters of *The Years With Ross*, from including in its entirety *The New Yorker* story that he had written about the opening of the St. George Hotel in Brooklyn, surely one of the least accomplished of his published writings, yet one which stood firmly in his mind as a high point in his career. At any rate, the blanks piece is mislaid and no longer available for later judgments.

I put the parody into the mail. Several days went by, more of an interval, perhaps, than what had followed my previous offerings. Then came a cautiously worded letter from Mrs. White: They would not be able to use the parody, but Mr. Ross would like to have a talk with me, to see me, in fact.

This was overwhelming news. No other work involvement of any kind could have appealed to me so mightily. A closer and more active relationship with *The New Yorker* seemed to hold every possibility that I could wish for: a great lift for my writing; money, certainly; and not least, the likelihood of an escape from the *Transcript*, its galling routines and diminishing wage.

The parody, in retrospect, did not belong in *The New Yorker*. There was no part of the magazine where it could have been accountable, without cumbersome explanations. It might have done very well in some other magazine, simply with the line, "With Apologies to *The New Yorker*," but I doubt that there was one which would have given this much recognition to Ross's thrusting new enterprise.

The two of my friends who knew most about *The New Yorker* were less enthusiastic than I had expected. Laurence Winship, then city editor of *The Boston Globe*, suggested that I was getting on well as a contributor and not to be in a hurry to make a change. Gluyas Williams, whose black-and-white drawings were as much in demand at *The New Yorker* as among newspaper syndicates, was sure that I should stay in Boston and keep on trying to write for Ross, and under no circumstances go to work in *The New Yorker* office. Neither Winship nor Williams could give me any clear reasons why I should be so cautious, and I think they were reluctant to discourage me by telling me the truth: that I should be venturing beyond my depth with an extraordinarily demanding and fastidious employer. They had at the same time, I think, too high a professional regard for Ross to be willing to blame him for what might happen to me. McCord thought it a great chance for me to get ahead in a hurry, and so did I. All I could see was the perfection of Ross's product from week to week. Nothing would have deterred me from seeking to become involved in it.

(Ross told me later of his great admiration for Williams. He was rejecting, he said, the advertising of a large company, because its copy was illustrated by a flagrant imitator of Williams' distinctive style. Ross said he had tried repeatedly to persuade Williams to join the staff but that Williams refused to work in New York or be on anyone's staff. "He's one of these goddam Bostonians," said Ross, with a kind of despairing approval.)

It was plain in any case that I ought to go down and see Ross. I believe it was Mrs. White who made the appointment, and it was as much for my convenience—or, rather, my necessities—as for Ross's: nine o'clock of a Sunday night, at *The New Yorker* office, which meant that I could catch The Owl and be back at my *Transcript* desk punctually at 8:15 on Monday.

My wardrobe presented a somewhat narrow choice for such a confrontation: the shiny blue serge from Filene's Automatic Bargain Basement, or a rather daring *fantaisie* that I had bought for a $10 bill at Max Keezer's, Harvard's celebrated secondhand man. This latter suit was a double-breasted affair which must have cost its initial owner a goodly sum. The cut was conservative, but the fabric was a one-of-a-kind importation, a rich green, flecked with brown in a diagonal weave, with an overplaid of large squares, picked out in hairline sky-blue thread—a country suit that sounds more alarming than it was. The coat was in good shape, although the sleeves were a bit short, but the great hazard to the wearer I discovered not at Max's but later on at home, when I happened to hold the trousers up to the light: the seat had worn gossamer thin. Through some miracle, no thread had let go in this cobweb-like area, but a stray splinter or even a sharp corner would wreck the whole project. It was nothing in which to lounge idly against *Transcript* furniture. I hoped it would hold together while more prosperous times caught up with me in New York.

I had no idea of what the scene would be at *The New Yorker* office of Harold Ross on a Sunday night at nine o'clock. Working Sundays or working nights seems ordinary to anyone who ever worked on a morning paper, and I expected vaguely to find some degree of staff operation going on, with people

pounding out copy on their typewriters and the general hubbub of production. The office hours and schedules of the place
were wholly unknown to me. I think I assumed that if Ross
were on the job at that hour, so would be his associates.

The day passed very slowly indeed. I had spent the night
at the Shelton, at the time a sort of deluxe Y.M.C.A. on Lex-
ington Avenue. Its upper rooms afforded a wide view of the
midtown skyline, and I mooned at the window for some time
before turning in, sharpening an awareness that I was about
to try to crack this neighborhood and wondering if I were
going to make it. I realized that I was striking the classic
posture for the circumstance: the early crisis for the hero of
a fiction work, surveying the battleground of his coming tri-
umphs and perhaps singling out the ultimate penthouse or
terrace apartment where he would eventually be living. It was
corny, I knew, but I let it run on. When the immediate present
seemed to warrant musings of such splendor, a man was reluctant to go to bed at all. By the time Sunday evening came,
I was in a fine old sweat.

Not a light showed in the windows of 25 West 45th Street
when I walked by a good half-hour before the time Ross had
fixed for our meeting. A lifelong habit of being much too
early was plaguing me, but I was afraid to present myself until
nine o'clock lest I interrupt some other engagement of Ross's.

The watchman got up from his desk in the dimly lit lobby
and unlocked the street door for me at 8:55. He wrote my
name and destination in his after-hours log. He believed Ross
was in his office, but he did not seem sure of it, and I marveled
at the stupidity of one who could be so uncertain of the where-
abouts of such a tenant as Harold Ross. The man must be
worse than illiterate, I thought.

The only light in the corridor where the watchman let me
out of the elevator came through a transom over a door at
the end. I began to think that I might have mistaken the

arrangements, but I went on down the corridor and knocked. The door opened instantly, and there was Ross. He was obviously alone in the small, starkly furnished office. Aside from the watchman, I am sure there was no one else in the building but ourselves.

Ross looked neater, somehow, than I had been led to expect. His hair, reported as always standing up in all directions, was decently brushed. His rumpled dark suit was nondescript, and he looked like a man who gave no thought whatever to his clothes; he did not have to, and he was not interested anyhow. His shoes, which were mentioned in all accounts of him, were in fact the high black shoes of the legend, with the upper part laced crosswise on hooks—a style which he subsequently abandoned. These impressions were gathered in the course of our interview, and I set them down simply for the record. I could hardly take them in at all, so instantly exciting, so arresting to me was everything about Ross: his words, his ideas, and the quick succession of emotions so visible in his extraordinarily mobile facial expressions. He was intense about everything and certainly one of the least long-winded of conversationalists. His manner to me was offhand and affable, and I immediately fell into the dangerous illusion that we had known each other for years and understood each other perfectly.

Although *The New Yorker* was growing and prospering, Ross began the conversation with an altogether gloomy recital of his problems, the lack of capable staff writers and assistants, his inability to cover all sorts of great subjects for want of the writer. For one story in particular that he was pursuing he could find no writer at all. "I'd get ———— for it," he said, naming a well-known woman novelist, "if she weren't such a squally old bitch." The idea of getting her had apparently just occurred to him, and, squally or not, he made a note on a memorandum pad.

Ross seemed so burdened by his troubles that I broke into a

vein of reassurance. I had indeed read every issue minutely, and I was chattering away about what I felt to be the magazine's virtues and how various weaknesses might be shored up when I noticed Ross eying me intently. I paused. "Goddam it," he said, "let *me* talk."

Of other statements of his that Sunday evening in the January of 1933, I can recall only two verbatim. One came in Ross's recollection of his own newspaper days, just before our entry into World War I, when he was beating his way East from Colorado as an itinerant reporter. "I worked on twenty-three papers in two years," he said. "If I stayed anywhere more than two weeks, I thought I was in a rut."

The main subject of the evening proved to be that Ross was offering me a job. This had seemed to be a probability, but I had thought there was a chance that he wanted to talk to me about my writing instead. Any sort of job with him was acceptable; I had never met anyone at all like Ross. He was insistent, to my surprise, that I regard it all as an experiment, a trial spin, and that I get a three months' leave of absence from the *Transcript* in case a permanent job was not warranted.

The leave of absence seemed to be absurd. I could see no likelihood of getting one at a time when employers welcomed almost any excuse to cut down the payroll. A job vacated was simply so much money saved; replacements lay in the misty future, when prosperity would somehow, of its own volition, return. But I could see no possible need of a leave; whatever work *The New Yorker* gave me, I was sure I could do. Ross simply did not realize how good I was.

Ross was firm about the leave. I should get a leave; my family would stay home during the trial period. He knew a great deal more about himself and his wants than I did. He was not running a school in which promising young men were brought along and promoted; neither was he hiring anyone as an encouragement. A perfectionist all the way, he was looking for a genius. He had three on the staff: James Thurber, E. B. White, and Wolcott Gibbs. These three could do just about any kind of work called for; they could do it quickly, brilliantly, each with an original resource of his own and all capable of satisfying Ross's exacting demands. They were the backbone of the staff that worked in the office. Ross had in addition such departmental writers and contributors as Alexander Woollcott, Robert Benchley, and Dorothy Parker. John Mosher, who reviewed movies each week, was an indispensable manuscript reader and editorial aide. Katharine White must have been the ideal editorial administrative Number Two for Ross; I am not sure what her precise title was, but her influence and taste were felt in all matters, and she worked successfully with Ross throughout his career.

These were all people of great ability. It never occurred to me that I was being examined as their possible equal, but this was always in the back of Ross's mind when he hired anyone; the odds seemed against it, the evidence was none too heartening, but he owed it to his cherished magazine and to his own peace of mind to find out whether some great new stride might be forthcoming from the recruit. So, if I did not realize what was vaguely expected of me, Ross did. He did not wish to uproot a Massachusetts family and a man with a job and cast them adrift in New York at the darkest point of the Depression. None of this was clear to me at the time. But it did appear that the leave was essential. I said I would try to arrange it.

Ross seemed relieved. He proposed to pay me $150 a week, which was almost four times my *Transcript* wage. That would be fine, I said. Our conversation ended at around 10:30. I would begin work two weeks later, provided, of course, I could have the leave of absence. Ross stood in the doorway as I went down the dark corridor to the elevator. His final utterance, shouted after me, seemed even more encouraging. "Goddam it, Morton," he said, "I don't want a hundred-and-fifty-dollar-a-week man. I want a three-hundred-dollar-a-week man!"

So infatuate was my frame of mind that I saw nothing of a warning in Ross's words. It would be a rather vertical rise for me, financially, I had to admit; in the several functions that I felt I could carry on, I could not think readily of a combination that would fetch any such salary. It began to enter, ever so slightly, my consciousness that I did not know exactly what I would be doing to earn my $150 a week, let alone $300, but I boarded The Owl filled with self-esteem and putting aside any misgivings as silly, if not downright cowardly.

Henry Claus, the editor of the *Transcript*, listened amiably to my story at the office the next morning. I did not work directly for him, but his was the decision that counted, and I knew it would be futile to ask the city editor for a leave of any duration. He would have refused it out of meanness alone, but Claus was a good editor and a good friend. Of course I should seize the opportunity, said Claus, and I was welcome to the leave. He knew perhaps better than any of us how badly the *Transcript* was faring; he would help a staff man into a better job, if he could, even though it might mean trouble and arguments for himself. The leave still seemed to me unnecessary, but Claus made the arrangements altogether painless. He said he would make it plain to the city editor.

As the interval before my departure went on, the question that friends kept asking me, and reasonably enough, began to haunt me: What will you be *doing* at *The New Yorker?* Ross had really given me no answer to that question, and I was so hopeful of the days ahead that the lack had not yet troubled me. It was when Karl Schriftgiesser told me the news staff was giving a farewell party for me that I felt the need, suddenly, of more precise job specifications. I had explained to everyone Ross' insistence that I was going on leave of absence and no more, but I think it was hard for any of us to believe that a

Transcript man who had been offered a new job, in times like those, would not manage somehow to hang on to it. Even so, the possibility of returning in defeat, after setting out from a farewell party, was appalling. I begged Karl to call it off. This particular departure was not the right occasion for a party, I argued.

Excuses for *Transcript* parties were all too few; there was no way of stopping this one. The hotel business was in anything but an arrogant mood in the Depression days, and someone from the *Transcript* must have put the arm, so to speak, on the Parker House with much conviction, for the management laid on a fine buffet. There was quite good gin, more than we could drink; the party was great fun; and I very nearly lost my misgivings in the wave of good feeling and alcohol. I cannot remember whether the disliked city editor came to the party. My impression is that he was invited and came; but he was so steadfast a chiseler that I am sure no want of an invitation would in itself have kept him away.

The New Yorker's office day began at 10:00 A.M., ending toward 6:00. I found that the hours, slightly later than the *Transcript's*, were taken by the staff at both places with equal gravity; the Thurber–White–Gibbs stratum arrived just as punctually as the others, and we seldom took the full hour for lunch. Ross was around the place at all times, rarely seen but constantly felt as an all-knowing presence, and it was much better for a man to be there than not, if Ross happened to want him.

I saw practically nothing of other contributors and writers while I was there, but the people who worked in the office were wonderfully friendly and helpful in trying to make a newcomer feel at ease. They were remarkably few in number, in comparison with the magazine's later roster: Thurber, White, Gibbs, who did most of the writing produced in the office and who were equally capable in editing, rewriting, condensing, and manuscript reading; Mrs. White, a first-class editor in her own right; Charles Cooke, the great fact-gathering legman who supplied much of the bizarre—and always true—detail for which the "Talk of the Town" stories became famous; Raymond Holden, whom I came to know scarcely at all, so heavily was he occupied with what I believe was the function of managing editor; Bernard Bergman, who seemed to be in charge of all dealings with me and who was also thought to be the managing editor, provided Holden wasn't; Miss Terry, the office manager, unfailingly efficient and good-humored; Whitaker, the make-up man, who was responsible for the final layout of text, drawings, and filler, widely regarded as just about the best in the business; and John Mosher, film reviewer and manuscript reader, with whom I was to share an office. Of all these, I believe the Whites and Miss Terry were still actively with the magazine some thirty years later.

What impressed me most, and still does in retrospect, was how the seemingly fragmented efforts of these diverse personalities were made to produce on schedule each week a perfect published result. An evening newspaper with four or five editions in the pre-radio days called for the maximum in speed and correctness, and even a monthly publication must live successfully with an inexorable calendar, but I doubt that anything else has quite the pace of a weekly meeting the requirements that Ross established for *The New Yorker:* prose of all sorts, ranging into multi-part articles of much complexity and controversial risk; comic art and captions; beautiful covers; the insistence on being topical and up-to-date, and on many occasions ahead of the daily press; reviews and departments; verse; and always the quest for more innovations, better quality, and fresh talent.

"The Madhouse on 45th Street" was a description of *The Yorker* frequently heard in the early years, but I believe most of its currency was among writers and newspaper people whose work had failed to commend itself to Ross. There was certainly no sign of the madhouse in the unparalleled success of his magazine through the very bottom years of the Depression and ever since.

John Mosher and I turned up at about the same time, shortly after 9:30, on my first Monday morning. I remember him as dark, aquiline, carefully dressed, and working in complete silence save for an occasional ejaculation of disgust when he found himself reading an exceptionally bad manuscript. He was the reader par excellence, needing only the few revelatory clues, all but instantaneous, to determine whether to go on or to give up. By late forenoon he would have worked his way through a tall pile of offerings, between fifty and a hundred, I judge, and he would then begin rereading his gleanings and writing them up for further comments by others.

Mosher was reading stories and articles. I would be reading, I learned, the short offerings for "Talk of the Town" pages— anecdotes, tips, oddities, and, to my amazement in this first experience as a manuscript reader, a large number of old jokes, many of them venerable classics, all masquerading as the bonafide personal experience or original invention of those who had sent them in. I suppose it is characteristic for a man to feel, at any given age, that his experience up to that time represents the total of all human enlightenment. Three years of news reporting had afforded me, I thought, a broad and detailed understanding of human depravity. But nothing had ever led me to expect such infamous cheating as some of our contributors were attempting. It was shocking.

My reading instructions were simple enough: any manuscript at all promising I would pass along to Bergman with a comment; to each of the others I was to clip a rejection slip, and on each slip, so Bergman suggested, write in long hand the word "Sorry" and scribble a meaningless initial beneath it. Mr. Ross, it was explained, felt this would lend a personal touch to the otherwise terse formality of the rejection slip. I followed this instruction in all cases, but it seemed to me a crazy idea at the time, and it still does: why express regret to would-be plagiarists and frauds?

The only other office duty assigned to me during those first two weeks was interviewing insistent strangers in *The New Yorker's* reception room. These callers were usually women who wanted to write something for the magazine and who, untroubled by any thought of trying to make an appointment, had dropped in and demanded to see The Editor—Ross, or whatever his name was. The visitor was angered at not seeing Ross, and my own arrival as a small-bore substitute always struck her as a calculated insult. Anyone who actually would see her, the visitor seemed to feel, was not worth talking to, but so great were her generosity of mind and devotion to her craft that she would rough in her project, even to such a nincompoop as now confronted her.

No part of the project was yet on paper, it transpired, and what the visitor wanted, before sitting down to her task, was assurance that *The New Yorker* was eager to have her go to work on it. And what, by the way, would be the fee? These women were almost an identifiable type—expensively dressed, not bad-looking, and confident that their personal charms would more than make up for any deficiencies that their nonexistent writings might prove to have. A conversation with one of them was an exercise in mutual frustration, both parties retiring in dudgeon.

None of this work was worth anything like the wage Ross was paying me. I was worried on that score but enjoying the place immensely, and I was somewhat cheered when Ross asked me to draw up a report on *The New Yorker's* book-reviewing, which at that time was undoubtedly the weakest department in the magazine. I spent about four days on this assignment, bringing to bear several pages of documentation on significant omissions, the somewhat unaccountable selection of books that were reviewed, tardiness in comparison with other publications, and similar ills. I am sure, today, that Ross was much more acutely aware of these failings that I was, analyzing as he did every line in every issue, but I believe he said something encouraging to me about the report. At any rate, in the spring of 1933 Clifton Fadiman took over the department, and Ross's troubles with that part of the magazine were over for the duration of Fadiman's ten years in charge of it.

I am frequently startled in retrospect by the enormous gap between my own ignorance on some given occasion and the confidence I had felt at the same time in the sophistication and the fund of experience which I was sure I possessed. I am still encountering reminders of my greenness on matters which, as a hard-working newspaperman, I felt that I understood as few others did. A glimpse that was afforded me of how the New York reporters dealt with city officials is a case in point.

The glimpse resulted from the only large assignment that fell to me at *The New Yorker*, an attempt by Ross to bring up to date the story of Sailors' Snug Harbor, a home on Staten Island for aged and indigent seamen. Endowment of the home came from a trust created in perpetuity by Captain Randall, a retired sea captain-turned-farmer, who left as its main asset his farm, which was to become valuable metropolitan real estate. Such buildings as Wanamaker's department store, the Brevoort and Lafayette hotels, and many apartment houses in the Washington Square area were built on Randall acreage, and the value of the trust—regarded by many lawyers as the very model of muddleheaded philanthropy—stood at somewhere around $15 million by the time of the '30s. There was simply more income pouring in on the trustees than the available supply of old salts, from a diminishing merchant marine, could reasonably consume.

The trustees were all *ex-officio* personages of the municipality: the rector of Trinity Church, the president of the chamber of commerce, as I recall them, and possibly the mayor or the governor of the state as well. These seemed to be mere background figures, and the administration of the properties was carried on by salaried managers. The whole subject had been a recurring Sunday story for decades, and I began my quest by getting a few photostats from the newspaper files in the periodical room of the Public Library.

Feature stories about Snug Harbor over the years were inevitably jocose: true or false, the idea of a handful of old sailors trying to live it up on the captain's excessively profitable endowment was too much fun to resist. All the principals, in consequence, with the exception of the superintendent of the home itself—a harmless institutional type who simply made do on whatever budget the managers allowed him—were extremely press-shy. Rumors of the managers' fat salaries, of low rents and boons granted to tenants, and the high cost per old salt per annum were blandly ignored. No, Mr. Blank had nothing to say and was not answering questions—end of interview.

My first need, plainly, was an up-to-date map and valuations of the Snug Harbor holdings. Bergman suggested that *The New Yorker's* City Hall man, whom I shall call Burton, could help me get the data from the city officials. Burton was covering City Hall for Hearst and doing odd jobs on the side for Ross; it seemed to me characteristic of Ross to have in his employ so tough and immediately effective an operator as Burton proved to be.

A quiet, wiry little man in a rumpled old suit, Burton was leaning back in a chair with his feet on a press-room desk when I came in one midafternoon. In its furniture the room was almost as ramshackle as the *Transcript* city room. The man to see, Burton told me, was the comptroller of the city of New York, who had charge of all valuations and such, and he would introduce me to the acting comptroller, whose name was Prial. I suggested that we ought to make an appointment, but Burton said it would not be necessary. We walked over to the Municipal Office Building and got off the elevator at an upper floor, where we found ourselves at the threshold of a vast waiting room.

Ranged around the room were perhaps fifty men and women, waiting despondently to see the great man. They looked as if they had been waiting for years and were expecting to keep on indefinitely. Getting to see Prial was obviously slow business, and I was not reassured by the greeting we received from the receptionist, an elderly Irishman, skinny and mean, the sort of underling who bullies in the name of his master wherever he thinks it safe. There was certainly nothing impressive in our appearance, and the receptionist made no attempt to hide his contempt as we approached his desk. He did not know Burton, and Burton omitted to identify either of us.

"Prial in?" demanded Burton.

This was absurd; the receptionist seemed hardly to know which of his many choices of squelch he might most enjoyably apply. He looked us up and down derisively. "Got an appointment?" he asked. We had none, but I was hardly prepared for Burton's answer, in a voice audible to the whole room.

"Get in there, you son of a bitch," said Burton, "and tell Prial that Burton wants to see him."

Even more unexpected—to me—was the behavior of the receptionist. He jumped to his feet, beaming. "Oh," he said, "are you newspapermen? Just one minute," and off he went on the run for Prial's office.

Prial appeared immediately in his office doorway with gestures of welcome, and the receptionist showed us in. He greeted Burton as if the Hearst reporter were a long-absent friend. He was equally solicitous, I might say almost anxious, about what I might be wanting. It would, he assured us, be ours for the

217

asking. He listened tensely as I recited my needs: the map and
a list of valuations of land *and* buildings. His relief, when he
finally realized that what I wanted was, after all, a bit of commonplace clerical work, was noticeable: Whatever we were, we
were not Trouble. He summoned secretaries, laid out the specifications, and asked me how soon I needed the material. A day
or two later would have sufficed, but Burton spoke up. Tomorrow morning at 10:00, he said. Nothing to it, said Prial, and
if the job called for some work that night, the map and list
would most certainly reach me the next morning at 10:00, and
so they did. What a milder approach might have yielded I do
not know, but Burton's particular style of toughness seemed to
be just right.

I am embarrassed by one other recollection of Jimmy
Walker's New York; it has to do with a racing tip for which
a profligate friend of mine told me he had paid $100. My feel-
ing was that it must be an awfully good tip, something really
dependable, to be worth $100, and I begged my friend to let
me in on it. For a time he refused; if the word got around, the
whole arrangement would be ruined, he said, but he finally
swore me to secrecy and named the horse—Buster Boy in the
first at New Orleans.

It seems absurd that I did not know where to find a bookie
in New York, but I did not. When I asked a friend at *Variety*
to direct me to one, he was incredulous. "Why, anywhere along
Forty-sixth Street," he said, with a wide gesture. "Anywhere at
all." I pressed him to be more precise, and he stepped out on the
sidewalk with me, pointing to several nearby cigar stores. "Any
one of them," he said. I picked the nearest.

The cigar store was so crowded I could barely squeeze inside.
A policeman in uniform kept bawling at the crowd, "Keep
moving, folks! Keep moving." I bought a $5 betting slip—
Buster Boy on the nose—and struggled through the crowd into
the back room, where a Morse operator shortly began to call the

race. Buster Boy, to my astonishment, finished out of the money, and a second uniformed policeman in the back room took up the cry, "Keep moving. Plenty of room if you just keep moving—"

With the Snug Harbor story to write, I spent three days in a series of false starts and heavy-handed lumps of composition, working at all hours, in *The New Yorker* office and in my pleasant room at an East 37th Street lodging house. I have never enjoyed writing a long article, which was always hard work for me and often unsuccessful; nor have I ever quite understood how one man can turn a set of facts into easy, persuasive reading while another, with the same material, becomes only a conscientious bore. A short piece, some 1,500 words, of light purport is the only kind of article in which I have ever felt at ease, and the more I pounded away at the Snug Harbor stuff, which was really quite a rich haul of absurdities, the more lugubrious the result seemed to be. But it was a test case for me, and I had to turn in a draft or assert my own defeat.

The draft was just as bad as I judged it to be. It came back to me with many queries and marginal comments. My second attempt was no better, I am sure, and a few days after I had finished it, Bergman stopped at my desk with these words, which I had sensed were impending but which I could scarcely bear to hear: "Mr. Ross thinks you should plan to go back to Boston when your three months are up."

Two or three weeks of my trial period remained. It was quite proper of Ross to give me that much notice. But I felt that every hour I remained was an intrusion: the undesired tyro overstaying his welcome, the failure who would not leave, a hanger-on, an object of pity. I was sending home $100 of my $150 salary each week, and I knew that the relapse to my *Transcript* earnings could be postponed, but I felt that I should vanish as

219

quickly as possible. I called the office boy, who distributed the pay envelopes, and told him that I was leaving and needed my pay. It was a Thursday, nearing noon. A marvelous contretemps ensued, putting the final seal on my embarrassment and self-disgust.

The office boy, who had been especially helpful to me during the previous weeks, brought me the pay envelope in a few minutes. I said good-by to Thurber, Gibbs, the Whites, and Miss Terry, and, returning to snatch my hat and coat, to John Mosher. A couple of hours later as I was packing my belongings and about to leave my lodging house for a Boston train, I was waited upon by the office boy who was in a great state of jitters. Ross had just told him that by leaving on Thursday instead of finishing the week I was beating *The New Yorker* out of two days' pay, and if I did not return the money, Ross was going to take it out of the office boy's pay, a calamitous prospect in 1932 for any office boy.

So, I was leaving not only as an incompetent but also as untrustworthy, if not downright dishonest. I reimbursed the office boy. I apologized to him. I hoped he would not think, I told him, that I had foreseen any such mix-up, but he was too relieved to get the money back to engage in any review of my motives. He thanked me enthusiastically.

At the *Transcript* the next morning, the city editor, as I had expected he would, blandly disclaimed any understanding that I had been away on a leave of absence and was entitled to return to my job. A firm word or two from Henry Claus ended this harassment, and I am still warmed by the recollection of Henry's unquestioning friendliness when that was what I needed more than anything else. I had difficulty in trying to explain to anyone what had gone wrong in New York, or even why I had not stayed on for the full period of my leave. As I look back on it, I am sure that the real cause of my trouble was quite commonplace, so much so in fact that I could not possibly have understood it at the time: Ross was simply not as tirelessly interested in me as I was.

Not until some ten years later did I see Ross again. The war had begun, and *The New Yorker's* indispensable John Mosher had recently died. I mention these unrelated facts as the basis of the response Ross made to my banal question on this occasion when we next saw each other. The response transmitted, in a few words, Ross's concept of his magazine, his own responsibilities to it, and its relationship to the rest of the world. The words could have come from no one else but Ross.

George Bye, the literary agent, and I were lunching at the Ritz grill. One table removed from us, I noticed as we sat down, was Ross, who gave us a friendly nod, greeted Bye, and to my pleased surprise recognized me after a decade that was altogether blank so far as I was concerned, and said, "Hello, Morton."

I had no wish to intrude on Ross and the beautiful woman with him, but I thought I ought to pay my respect to my one-time employer, so I went over to his table. He introduced me to the beautiful woman, his wife. *The New Yorker* was of course in great shape as usual, but I could think of nothing but to mumble an inquiry about how things were at the magazine.

Ross shook his head. "Terrible," he said. "It's all shot to hell. Here is this goddam war," he went on, "and the staff are all trying to get into it. They're joining everything, even the goddam Air Force." This last, he seemed to feel, was unpardonable, but still worse was to come. "Those that aren't leaving me to *join* something," Ross concluded, "are dying on me."

Perhaps because he expected *The New Yorker* to lose all its staff writers and contributors to the armed forces, Ross asked me to send him something, and I sold him two or three pieces during the next few years. On being especially impressed by a Wayward Press article by A. J. Liebling, I wrote Ross a letter in praise of the department, and I happened to mention in it a sardonic piece by Nunnally Johnson, "An Open Letter to Criminals," which *The New Yorker* had published in its early years. I closed my letter with the suggestion that Ross need not trouble himself to reply to it. He answered it promptly with a word of thanks, but the fact was that the department, his letter continued, had never come anywhere near achieving the success that he had hoped for it. As for Nunnally Johnson—who had been for many years the most highly paid and successful screen writer in Hollywood—poor Johnson had fallen victim to the "diamond merchants," as Ross called the studio chiefs, and one got the impression from the letter that Johnson had just about dropped out of sight altogether, in choosing to write for the films instead of *The New Yorker*.

An invitation to *The New Yorker's* 25th Anniversary party in 1950 brought me to quite the finest evening occasion I ever expect to attend: about 500 of the magazine's staff and contributors, at a sort of glorified all-night dinner party in the ballroom of the old Ritz Carlton, laid on with all the style for which that hotel was renowned, beginning at nine o'clock and lasting indefinitely. The refreshments were offered at small tables for four or six, where the guests sat down whenever they felt like it and ordered whatever their fancy suggested.

I had wondered how Ross, who detested large gatherings and formality, would be taking his role of host, but I think I prefer to remember him as he was that night: the fond shepherd of this extraordinary flock of writers, artists, poets, critics, as many women as men among them, and most of them, including the celebrated, owing to Ross the discovery and encouragement of their larger talents. Throughout the evening he remained the gay and available master of these revels, able to call by name offhand every one of his charges, and even allowing himself, one felt, a trace of categorical pride in what guests a quarter-century of his editing could produce for a birthday blowout;

but any such attitude would have been improbable in Ross, for his true pleasure lay in what these people supplied for his magazine rather than any awareness of his own part in the transaction. It was a marvelous party. Although the crowd had thinned out somewhat by the time I left, the starchy red-liveried Ritz waiters were laying fresh tablecloths and place settings and taking orders as attentively as they had hours earlier; the ashtrays were kept emptied and polished; the champagne flowed undiminished; and the toast under a bit of Lobster Newburg was hot and crisp as always. In the succession of wonderful conversations with others at the party I am not sure when it was that I said goodnight, but I believe it was about 4:00 A.M.

●●●

Escape from the Transcript

THE BOSTON EVENING TRANSCRIPT, by early 1936, was going into the first of many convulsions of ownership and policy which occupied the five years before its death in 1941. Its president and proprietor, George S. Mandell, died suddenly in 1935, and for some months none of us had any idea of who owned the paper or headed the company until a wealthy Boston business-man, an accredited Brahmin, came in one day and began giving peremptory, if somewhat piffling, orders to Henry Claus. Word of this got quickly about the office, but no one knew whether he had become the principal stockholder, or was acting for the mortgage holders, or was simply a rich and convincing nut, a not unlikely role for a Bostonian of his status and vintage.

The position of this magnifico in the *Transcript* was of some interest to the staff, for not long after his first descent on us he set out on a grand tour of Europe and began sending back ac-counts of his travels to Claus. They were addressed to "Editor," and it was plain that they were intended as something more than mere greetings from overseas: it looked ominously as if the sender expected them to be published in the *Transcript*.

The letters were, unintentionally of course, high comedy. The Late George Apley in John Marquand's novel wrote similar

224

letters to his family, from London: It was much like Boston, only there was more of everything. Two of our man's findings reported from Rome were that the Colosseum was really not very different from Soldiers' Field, the Harvard stadium, while the celebrated Capitoline Hill had a good deal to put him in mind of our Beacon Hill, and so on.

It was one thing to work for a paper that was running out of funds, to skimp, extemporize, and struggle to keep up a journalistic standard, but it was quite another to expect such an editor as Henry Claus to put letters like these into the *Transcript*. The paper would look as if it had lost its wits. I believe it was the late James Ernest King, the chief editorial writer, who devised the elegant face-saver. The letters would be run inside, under a news head and possibly only in the first of our three editions, and preceded by an editorial note somewhat as follows: "This is the first of a series of letters just received from Mr. Blank B. Blank, who is traveling in Europe. Mr. Blank is one of the principal stockholders of *The Boston Evening Transcript*."

The first real casualty of this new pseudo-regime was the man who had become our combined managing editor, city editor, copyreader, and, in a pinch, rewrite man. He was the only staff member with a background of good newspaper experience elsewhere.

Newspapers at the time, even the more sensational, usually turned away from putting into print the term "sexual intercourse," preferring so ornamental a substitute as "intimate relations," which could, after all, mean nothing more extreme than a first-name basis. "Improper relations" was another standby bit of language—bottom-pinching? A kiss in the dark? "Assault" could be almost anything, yet it had a style-book status with many deskmen.

The upset point for the *Transcript* came in an out-of-town murder case that I was covering, when the prosecutor asked "the other woman" whether the defendant had engaged with her "in sexual intercourse." I included the question in the long exchange of questions and answers that I was filing with an old Western Union telegraph operator. About half an hour later the messenger boy handed me a note that I was wanted on the telephone. The managing editor, in a state of some tension, was asking if I was sure that I had quoted the prosecutor precisely. I told him the court stenographer would confirm the language. Was I sure? Certainly.

"Good." The managing editor sounded much relieved. It was approaching three o'clock, and our final edition was about to close. Then, with a damn-the-torpedoes air, he said, "I'm going to run it that way."

His decision pleased me. I seconded it heartily. Let the Nice Nellies tremble in their beds.

There was much favorable comment on the *Transcript's* boldness by others covering the trial when the evening papers reached us at our hotel. None of the other papers had mentioned "sexual intercourse"; it was as if the *Transcript* had accomplished a coup of some consequence, but our prestige lasted only overnight.

Midway through the next morning's session, the boy handed me a message: File no more copy and return to the office immediately. The managing editor was fired out of hand and had left by the time I got back that afternoon. For the rest of the trial the *Transcript* used the AP. The managing editor was, I think, part of a clearing out of the *ancien régime*, and this excuse—extremism—was as handy as any other for getting rid of him. We had, I found, a new "publisher"—a title which no one had seemed to hold up to that time—and a news editor who was taking charge of everything but the editorial page, which Henry Claus continued to conduct and which was about the only redeeming feature the paper had left. Several reporters and deskmen were let out for reasons of economy, local news all but vanished, and page one became largely an assortment of odds and ends from the AP. It was the beginning of the most disagreeable interval in my experience, lasting some six months and ending on a hot Saturday morning in August, 1936, with a delicious abruptness.

The *Transcript* itself had been declining more severely than the rest of the business community. Two circumstances, nevertheless, served to gloss over the poor prospects: the fantastically rich entertainment afforded by the daily round of a news reporter, and the advent of the New Deal and its impresario, Mr. Roosevelt. News reporting was a great pastime, but the pay was too little, and I found myself yearning to become involved in the surpassing novelties proliferating so grandly in Washington. How or with whom I could not quite envision. After all, what was my credential other than a few years of work, at a declining wage, on a paper that had never in its life backed a Democrat? To point with pride to my brief interval at *The New Yorker* would be like the student from India who boasts in his *curriculum vitae* that his work for a Harvard or Oxford degree ended in failure.

The only close friend that I had in a New Deal agency was Robert E. Huse, who was about to move to Washington to help John G. Winant set up the administration of the newly enacted social security programs. Bob and his family we had met quite by chance; they had proved to be our next-door neighbors in a Cambridge apartment house, and we all had found many interests and pleasures together through the years that followed. A New Hampshire Yankee who had worked for the Frank Knox paper in Manchester and for the Associated Press, Bob was highly regarded by Winant; he was among the first score or two of the key people picked by Winant for an agency which came to number tens of thousands of employees. As for Winant himself, the lanky, Lincolnesque young former governor of New Hampshire, there was no personality in Washington for whom

I would have gone to work with more gusto. He had an extraordinary power of making people feel that they ought to try to help him.

Bob was as close to being a ground-floor connection with a nascent New Deal agency as I could have wished. He was buying in on a nuisance in trying to help me, but he said to me, just as he was leaving for Washington in 1935, "Don't worry. I'll get you the kind of job you ought to have." My own bid to Bob for an escape from the *Transcript* was that I would take anything—running an elevator or opening mail—anything at all.

I can think of few more nagging tasks than filling out application forms for employment by the federal government. By mailing the forms to Bob for expert examination, I was able to retrieve my errors of omission and insufficiency until, in the course of six or eight months, I had brought together enough sanguine interpretations of my meager occupational past to make a faintly affirmative impression on a hasty reader. The great stumbling blocks were an almost total absence of what the U.S. Civil Service Commission regarded as "educational qualifications," and my failure to have had sole authority over and responsibility for and to have directed the work of large numbers of my fellowmen. In simple truth, I had always worked for someone else and never with so much as a secretary to direct and be authoritative about. My previous employment was supposed to have been not only continuous but also "progressive" —hardly the term for a long downhill trend in the *Transcript's* payroll.

The general custom of the period was that any young man who was not in college got a job and went to work unless he had a great deal of money. Not wishing to return to college for my sophomore year in the fall of 1919, I had gone to work in my father's hardware business. I had stayed in it quite without progress for eight years. I could hardly expect the Civil Service Commission to understand why I had thought Williams College a complete waste of time and why being a clerk in a hardware store had been so much better than completing three more years there. I thought it absurd to believe that more of the life of a Williams undergraduate would have augmented my usefulness to the Social Security Board, but I was bound to admit that my total offer must have looked pretty thin.

The fruits of my news reporting were old clippings from the *Transcript*. Nothing is worse than a news clip to present as proof of anything more than the mere enployment itself. A self-contained masterpiece might help, but most news writing has to be judged by many extrinsic values: the time available for getting and writing or dictating the story, the risks and difficulties of the occasion, how the work compared with that of competitors, and how many faint hearts among his superiors the reporter had to persuade in order to get it into print at all. Few of these considerations show through to the stranger who reads the clip. Worst of all, the more formidable the local reasons for developing the story and printing it at some length, the more trifling it may seem to one who thinks all news begins and ends in New York or in the mimeographed releases from prime ministers in world capitals.

My clippings were no more impressive than my one year of college. I was not even a veteran, and this at a time when Veterans' Preference was supposed to put, automatically, at the top of a Civil Service list of eligibles, those veterans who had merely passed the examination, no matter how high the grades of the non-veterans might be. I doubt the principle was consistently applied, especially in higher strata, but it was a handy dodge for the commission and the politicians to invoke in filling a job or keeping someone out of it. My own application, after months of suspense, was firmly turned down.

The job I was trying to get had many virtues. It would be in the New England regional office of the Social Security Board in Boston, as representative of the board's informational service. The work involved all publicity and information necessary for the launching of federal old-age insurance, unemployment compensation, and the three big federal-state public assistance programs for the aged, dependent children, and the blind. Some nineteen million wage earners were affected by old-age insurance alone. Many novel federal-state relationships would be coming into being, while the political temper of the six states ranged from one-party Republicanism in Maine and Vermont to one-party Curleyism in Massachusetts.

My friend Bob Huse caused me to meet John Pearson, another trusted aide of John Winant's, who was to be the board's regional director for New England and who was also determined that I should be the information and publicity man. Some interim cheer came shortly afterward when the Civil Service Commission informed me that I had been accepted as "acting" representative on a purely temporary part-time basis, to be paid by the hour on a voucher system so cumbersome that I turned in only enough to indicate that I was indeed "acting." The regional office consisted at the time of Pearson, myself, two stenographers, a switchboard that none of us knew how to operate, several suites of vacant rooms, and, roughly, a desk and a couple of chairs for each of us. Pearson, I soon found, was a genuine virtuoso in the art of public administration. It would take a long string of adjectives to describe him: courageous, tenacious, honest, generous, determined to help his associates do their best, intuitive and intelligent, extraordinarily farsighted. He was, into the bargain, a man of sound risibilities and a gay companion.

My status as "acting" became the more tantalizing as Pearson and I began sizing up the work to be done during the first years of getting the federal insurance programs started. More permanent arrangements had to be made. The Civil Service people were still stand-offish, and I decided to confide my problem to an old friend, Elizabeth Eastman, who had once described herself to me as a "one-woman lobbyist." She was a sister of Joseph B. Eastman, the chairman of the Interstate Commerce Commission, and it was her pleasure to take a hand in any sort of occasion or hearing in Washington where she thought her advice would be useful. Her gentle, soft-voiced manner, white hair, and slight figure gave the impression of an amiable young grandmother or elder aunt, but she knew everyone and everything in the government, and she was immensely respected by the more permanent administrative personnel. She sent me back a pleasant note, and said she would see what she could do.

The *Transcript* closed at 1:00 on Saturdays. It was a dull day and approaching noon when the office boy laid a telegram on my desk. It told me I had received a permanent appointment as the New England representative of the informational service and bade me report in Washington Monday to begin a basic-training course. Claus was out. We were paid for the week on Fridays. No one kept anything in his desk worth having. I was out of the office in seconds, running for the last time down the long flight of stairs to Washington Street, where the erroneous old brass plate, surviving other changes, continued to misinform the stranger: "Editors Two Flights—Reporters Three Flights."

I telephoned Claus my farewell at his home that evening. He seemed as pleased as I was over the great escape. He made a handsome escape of his own not long afterward and became publisher of a paper in Wilmington, Delaware, at a salary approximating the *Transcript's* total editorial payroll. The story goes that his wife came home late one afternoon, just after he had received word of his new position, and found Claus methodically smashing into a trashcan a dozen or more empty milk bottles which had been awaiting return to the market for refund. She remonstrated, at which Claus announced, "Neither of us is ever to return another bottle for a refund for the rest of our lives."

231

●●

CHAPTER SIXTEEN

Working for the Government

I NEVER FOUND OUT what had finally moved the Civil Service Commission to accept me, but I believe Bob Huse and Elizabeth Eastman talked to the skeptics and carried the day. I believe, too, that the qualifications laid out for the informational jobs had been so highfalutin, envisioning a kind of journalist-editor who was also an accredited social worker and chamber of commerce promoter, that no one came along who could meet them. If the Civil Service had been straining at a gnat in my case, it had surely swallowed a few camels in some of the new colleagues I met that Monday morning. Much of this impression was due to the assortment of personalities and behavior when strangers from one end of the land to the other are suddenly put to work together, but I do recall a senator's mistress, queening it behind her mascara, a putative relative or two of other senators, and an occasional big figure from the American Legion. Even so, it was an eager group, full of curiosity and belief, and achieving, in the event, a remarkably successful result.

I learned early that it was bad form to ask anyone where he was from. One could ask almost anything else, but a good half of the recruits seemed to become flustered and unresponsive to

232

even the idlest questions on this subject. It reminded me of the two confidence men in the O. Henry story, one of whom identifies himself as hailing from "the Mississippi Valley," at which the other invites him to look in if he is ever "on the Pacific Coast." The reticence in the Washington group, I learned, came from the fact that many had not lived in the city where they were to be stationed, and they dreaded outcries and political wire-pulling from the local aspirants if this were emphasized: the less said about it the better.

It seems absurd that responsible adults should be troubled by such cares, but I soon realized that administrative circles in Washington were a vast whispering gallery through which the wildest rumors—usually having to do with some drastic and supposedly imminent interference with the agency by Congress —were always rocketing. The old-timers ignored rumor, but the newcomer was less assured, having yet to learn that though the power of Congress was vast, so was its inertia. Since we were all newcomers, we tended to believe almost everything we heard, as well as some of the singular preconceptions we had brought along with us to Washington.

Our rosiest illusion, which seemed to be shared by everyone from top to bottom in our very new organization, was that we were not going to become encumbered by "red tape." We were not quite sure what that meant, but red tape was, vaguely, too much system, too many steps to be taken before something could be done. Red tape was all very well for the stuffy, old-line agencies—Treasury, Post Office, and such—but we were modern, we felt: energetic, quick, decisive, determined to get on with the work itself and not to be slowed by mere methodology.

Paperwork would be held to the minimum. Here, too, were great programs dealing with people, with human beings, and not with commodities or finance or mines or waterways. So, all would come down to the grass-roots level, where the people were, the only sensible policy in a nation whose grass

233

roots varied so widely. Instead of a centralized control in Washington, far from the real pulse of American life, the agency's field organization would be the dominating force; Washington would be available, of course, to offer discreet advice and information—if we wanted it—but we should all be going out virtually on our own, each to be meeting in his own way the needs of his own particular kind of grass roots.

No more agreeable attitudes than these could be expressed to a green staff about to go out on field jobs. Naturally we preferred to believe in them; in fact, it embarrasses me to remember how many odd and impossible ideas I accepted unquestioningly during those first weeks in Washington.

I was hardly prepared for the velocity of the basic-training course. The informational service occupied our first Monday with an all-day meeting. The Washington staff explained their work and ours, and we were given schedules of the lectures and seminars that were to fill the next six weeks. From the next day on, our sessions began as early as 8:00 in the morning and lasted until 6:00, sometimes running on into an evening when the lecturer was not available earlier. It was the most concentrated intake of information in my experience, before or since, bringing us a brilliant succession of experts on every aspect of the program—law, economics, public welfare, pensions and insurance, government, industry—and with it all we were drilled daily in every line and word of the Social Security Act itself, what it meant and what it did not mean. In point of getting its money's worth, the basic training course was about as good an investment by a government agency as I could imagine. I recall not a single speaker of the scores who talked to us who was not interesting and well on top of his assignment. I had not worked so hard and so uninterruptedly since I was a schoolboy.

The group with whom I entered the course, numbering forty to fifty men and women from all the various bureaus and departments of the Social Security Board, were excellent company, bright, lively, and friendly. With no more than some 200 of the professional and executive staff as yet on the job, no social stratification, no hierarchy according to official status had developed. Almost all of us were on a first-name basis immediately; no one was on the way up or the way down; friendships came readily. It was too soon to decide who was Important or where the center of gravity lay among the bureaus, and in truth I believe most of us were too inexperienced to have sensed the ever-shifting caste system in federal employment. We looked askance at the old-line agencies, and we realized dimly that they felt the same way about us. We tended to huddle together in our newness, with the result that morale was high.

Of all the recollections of meeting so many strangers in that summer of 1936, the one most clearly in my mind is certainly, also, the most trivial. Some of the training-course group went on to distinguish themselves, and two or three reached positions of great prestige in public service. But most of them are blurred for me today with the exception of one man, a pleasant, well-turned-out Middle Westerner, perhaps four or five years older than I was, who invited me to his small apartment one evening for a drink before dinner.

We were in the kitchen, and while he was setting out glasses and a bowl of ice, I undertook to refill the ice trays. I was just sliding one back into the freezing compartment when I heard anguished shouts from my host in the next room. "Don't do that! *Don't do that!*" Out he came on the run, and I am not exaggerating when I say he was in a state of near-hysteria, panting and sputtering with concern. I could not imagine what was troubling him so.

"*Never,*" he said to me as he seized the tray I was holding, "*never* put a tray back *like that!*" He snatched a dish towel from the rack and wiped off the bottom of the tray. "If you don't wipe the bottom first," he said, "it will *stick.*"

I do not know the origin of my host's trauma on ice-tray

techniques, but he certainly transferred it to me. Not that I was such a sloppy operator myself; I could strip off bottom drops with the best of them. But I don't believe I have ever refilled an ice tray in all the years since without thinking of the man and his alarm, and wondering what ruthless discipline had imposed it on him. I have forgotten whether old-age insurance benefits were provided by Title II or Title VII of the Social Security Act, but on ice trays I have total recall.

By the time the basic-training course ended and I got back to Boston, the regional office had expanded considerably. All the bureau representatives were on the job, some with assistants. We had an auditor, an attorney, and—most usefully—an executive assistant, who was the only genuine old-government-hand in the place, a harried but pleasant man in his early thirties who knew every form and regulation in the appallingly complex process of getting anything done in a government office. His name was Henry Thurston, and he was so intensely the professional at times that one could not resist giving him a workout.

Other than rail transportation and a $5-a-day living allowance when away on business, I had no authority to make expenditures. For the entire needs of the regional office, we learned eventually, a petty-cash fund of something like $50 or perhaps $100 every three months was provided. Yet I would receive from time to time urgent telegrams ordering me to rush photographs or copies of some publication to Washington. These I simply ordered after asking the price, and told the trusting supplier to send the bill to the regional office for my attention.

A bill for some pathetically small amount would reach me a few days later. I made it a point not to give Thurston any advance explanation of the purchase, and I simply scrawled an "OK" or "Approved" on the bill, signed my name, and sent it along to him. It never failed to strike fire. Minutes later, perhaps accelerated by a knowing office messenger, the bill was flung down on my desk, and there was Thurston, bursting with procedural data. The conversation was always much the same.

"What is this 'Approved' supposed to mean?"

"Why, just that—I ordered the stuff, it was delivered, and the price is correct. Naturally, I approved it."

"But this approval is not worth the paper it's written on. You haven't any authority to approve bills."

"I know that very well."

"Then why do you send me this?"

"I want you to get it paid."

"But you didn't follow procedures."

"There wasn't time."

"I'm not going to pay it."

"It will look mighty queer when this poor damn little photographer tells the papers that he can't collect seven dollars and ninety-three cents owed him for materials supplied in good faith to the U. S. Social Security Board in Washington, D.C. You have the correspondence on it."

"Oh, give it here."

Our regional attorney was something else again. He was a South Boston Irishman, phenomenally hirsute, squat, heavy, but airily light of foot when dancing a jig or a reel under the alcoholic drive of a Christmas office party, when he would also give rather long recitations and sing old-time ballads. His appearance, as he peered out at the world from under immensely bushy eyebrows, was forbidding, but he was a harmless chap, a small-time police-court lawyer whose main ambition was to be a judge on the federal bench.

I suppose the attorneys—we kept getting more and more of them—were the most dispensable members of the regional staff. They really had nothing to do, for the brave visions of the decentralized agency, guided from the grass roots, never gained the least substance. Any legal determination, however unimportant, was made in Washington, yet additions to our attorney's staff kept appearing unexpectedly, and office space had to be found for them. If I looked in on the attorney to say good morning, there were always several lawbooks open on his desk. He would lay aside his morning paper, chat affably, and, just as I was leaving, pick up his diary and begin writing in it. He confided in me one morning why the diary was so important.

"When you and I have a talk like this," said the regional attorney, "I always put down in my diary, 'Conference with regional representative, informational service,' and I note the time and the subject of our consultation. I do it with everybody who comes in here—telephone calls, too." I would be surprised, he went on, by how big the totals become in the course of a month. "It makes a great impression on Washington in my monthly report."

The regional attorney was a great word-scrambler, given to adding or dropping out a syllable in many common words. It came to be considered quite high style by the staff to respond to him at a meeting with one or another of his own metamorphoses. A staff man would say, for example, that he was going to call on one of our "suburbuan" offices, while the next might announce that he was about to make up an "itinary." This last was so popular that we began using it not only at meetings but also among ourselves, and it even carried over at times into conversations with outsiders. Of all his inventions, that which lingers most fondly in my mind was the statement that he would take the matter up with "my fellow colleagues."

Just to brighten his day once in awhile, I used to ask the regional attorney to read some letter that I was about to send. It always pleased him and evoked from him intricate pronouncements on all manner of legal pitfalls. But it would start him musing on the desirability of setting up a general review of all correspondence going out of the office, under, of course, his own supervision, and it was not altogether safe to encourage

238

new ambitions in one already so crammed with them. Boston politics was his passionate hobby, and he was lost in his thoughts when I dropped in on him on the morning after Maurice J. Tobin, still in his thirties, had been elected mayor of Boston. It was a great upset; the attorney was actually talking to himself about it. "What an opportunity," he kept saying. "What a magnificent opportunity, and for such a young man!"

"How do you mean?" I asked him. "Is it really that good?"

"Why," said the attorney, "the honest graft alone is worth a quarter of a million a year."

"What's the 'honest graft'?"

The attorney was like a patient teacher giving a simple explanation to a backward child. "The insurance kickbacks," he said, "the insurance kickbacks alone . . ." His voice trailed off dreamily. "What a chance for a young fellow . . ."

Making speeches appealed to the regional attorney even more than politics. He was incurably the orator; of non-stop capacity, he would have been a real anchor man in any long filibuster. Our speaking engagements were intended to provide information about the Social Security Act and its workings, and to this end the regional attorney was booked to address a breakfast meeting at a convention of the National Association of Morticians. I wrote a tight fifteen-minute text for him and went along to hear him deliver it before some 500 delegates in the ballroom of the Statler Hotel. The speech was supposed to be a sort of *divertissement*, a transitional filler between the last of the breakfast coffee and the opening of the day's convention business; there was a firm understanding that it would begin and end on schedule.

I had an uneasy feeling that the attorney might be tempted to add a few flourishes of his own, for he had seemed rather offhand about it all when I gave him the text. On our way to the meeting I cautioned him about the time: essential, I said, to stay within our fifteen-minute allotment.

239

I turned the attorney over to the chairman and took a seat near the door. The next forty minutes were as grueling for me as any that I can recall. Far from embellishing the fifteen-minute text, the attorney discarded it altogether and was off on his own—all the way. He began with the historical significance of Boston as the seat of revolt against the cruelty and oppression of British rule, and it was a good quarter-hour before he reached the War of 1812—the wretched British once again. He was somewhere around Appomattox when the chairman got up and whispered to him at some length. The attorney nodded, reassuringly, and broke into a rousing endorsement of Woodrow Wilson, to be followed, one could sense, by the achievements of an even greater Democrat.

The whispered warning was not going to be heeded. Of that I was certain. There was, in fact, no way of stopping the attorney that I could imagine, and I think the chairman must have realized this. His remedy was a masterpiece.

The chairman went to the speaker's side and, not appearing to do so with any violence, simply edged him firmly away from the lectern—and the microphone—right in the middle of a sentence, and superseded him there. "I am sure we are all grateful to the speaker," said the chairman in ringing tones, "for giving us so generously . . ." etcetera, etcetera. There were a few hasty handclaps. I ducked outside to wait for the attorney. Not a syllable had been uttered on his main subject, the Social Security Act.

The attorney was in a great state of exaltation when he joined me a moment later, still transported by the sound of his own voice. "How did I do?" he asked me.

There was no use rowing about it after the fact. Nothing would ever make the attorney any different from what he was. I could only stay clear of his speechmaking in the future. At the moment, he would have taken it as a matter of course if I had told him it was the most wonderful speech I had ever heard in my life. "Fine," I said. "Everything was fine, but I think you talked a little too long."

The regional attorney was incredulous. "What the hell—" he said. "I stopped when they told me to, didn't I?"

He never fulfilled his ambition to be a federal judge. I doubt not that he would have made it had he lived, but he dropped dead of a heart attack some years later. It must have been a joyous end, for he died while in full flight, doing what he loved to do more than anything else: making a speech on a public platform.

We were not long in finding out that most government activities must be recorded; it is not sufficient, that is, to do the work; in addition, a report of it, with carbons on papers of various colors, must be filed. The report, often enough, took more time than the work did. It sounds like a cumbersome way of doing things, which of course it is; but two circumstances make it unavoidable: bigness, causing the disappearance of personal relationships in operations involving such huge staffs and expenditures; and the profound mistrust existing between Congress and the government agencies. Size alone has created similar ills for big business, but dependence on Congress puts its own freaky twist on how a government office must be. It is the fault not of either but of both; each expects the other to cheat. The agency asks for more money than it needs; Congress responds by an uninformed and heavy cut in the appropriation.

Somewhere in between, with just enough information and prestige to keep the transaction in the realm of feasibility, however high the amounts wasted, is the Bureau of the Budget. Underfinanced and understaffed, the Bureau purports to study the agency's needs and advise Congress on a reality somewhere between the request and the proposed cut. One is tempted to envision an all-powerful Bureau of the Budget, whose findings would be based on a true understanding of what is needed and what is unnecessary—an attractive idea if enough selfless supermen could be found to run it.

Our own people in Washington, for instance, called a series of meetings toward the end of our first year. A well-filled three-day session would have been enough, but for a time we were shuttling back and forth almost every week and seeming to develop little to show for it. We learned eventually that we were using up a modest unexpended balance which otherwise would have remained a surplus in our travel budget, and this, it was explained, would have embarrassed the whole chain of functionaries who had made and approved the original request, as well as all in Congress who had been parties to so heinous a deed: giving the power-crazed bureaucrats even more than they could squander. Better to end with a small deficit than any hint of surplus, or we might never get any more travel money at all.

The report—daily, weekly, monthly—makes the public employee live, I found, in a perpetual world of overstatement. It must prove, in the first place, not only that he was alive and on the job on this date or that but also that his accomplishments were as those of ten. For statistical returns, a form with various headings to be filled in was customary; but beyond this some long general statement, or boast, was usually wanted, and the longer the better. The long report meant that the work had been done thoroughly; its length also gave its author a chance to bury well down in it anything that might be especially controversial.

One of the statistical marvels that I recall turned up in a Washington meeting when a report was read showing that a regional representative had held some 900 "informational interviews" in a week, while doing all his other work in addition. He was asked about it somewhat pointedly, and he explained that the figure was the estimated number of delegates at a convention where he had made a speech. A speech was much more informative than an interview, he contended.

242

The long report was at the opposite extreme from boasting when there was something to be played down. In one of the federal-state programs, a nasty situation of illegality became known, and the bureau representative went to the state capital to look into it. He asked me to read his report, and after two pages of single-spaced odds and ends I found the nub of it in the middle of the third page. Any reviewer in Washington would have tired by that time, and it would have taken a very keen reader indeed to find cause for alarm in the bland, carefully hedged statement of the facts so briefly put.

I asked him why he had not made the matter the subject of his report and begun with a more emphatic reference to it. His explanation discouraged me, but from his point of view it had considerable force: the dirty end of the deal in the state office was being supported by political power of consequence, and further, he had reason to believe the situation was not altogether unknown to Washington. His mention of it, even half concealed and mild as it was, would keep him in the clear if trouble did come. "Why should I be the one to stick my neck out?" he said. If the situation continued, he could protect himself in future reports simply by referring cryptically to the dates of his previous reports on the same subject, in the certainty that no one would take the trouble to look them up and find out what he was talking about.

The demand for reports and paperwork seemed to be largely an attempt at self-justification by the agencies and their bureaus against that awful day of wrath when Congress would suddenly snatch off the lid from the Ant Palace and demand to know of every ant, from chiefs to supervisors on down to the lowliest: Where were you on October 23, what were you doing, and why were you doing it? The day never comes, but meanwhile, the reports multiply, and so do the people who are hired to read them, and the people who must then analyze the digests, and so on. By the time these documents have settled down in the files, the people concerned in them have gone somewhere else, the law has been amended, and the agency's great friends, or enemies, in Congress are off on the hustings trying to get themselves re-elected.

The writing style that I began to affect marks my first year with the government as among the outstanding jackass periods of my life. I have in mind the appalling mixture of governmentese and legal jargon which took over my attempts to answer inquiries from the public and which loaded office reports and most exchanges with Washington with an overpoweringly high-toned imitation of what I supposed to be the going thing in official prose. Oddly, I managed to keep news releases and speeches and radio texts in reasonably plain English, but the rest of what I wrote was pure rubbish. It puzzled me why I should have fallen into a vein so artificial and so unproductive. On mulling it over, I believe I found the cause.

Messages to Washington were, for instance, couched in an ornate third-person form, with much scrollwork: "It is respectfully requested that . . ." or "The informational service representative wishes to inform the director that . . . ." This was, of course, nonsense, but I think it was an attempt to eliminate any personal quality in my language that might embarrass my friend Bob Huse or make it seem as if I were trading on his friendship in any given situation, for it was he after all who had really got me the job. I suppose a case could be made out, for just such reasons, for a third-person way of life in the government service, but I must say it is more fun to work with people you like and trust and to treat each other accordingly.

The legalistic spree that must have made most of my letters unintelligible was due simply to greenness. It faded away as I gained experience and under the kindly nudging of John Pearson, the regional director, and his question: "What is the use of sending a man a letter that he cannot possibly be expected to understand?"

We were so stuffed, for a time, with the social security law itself that we tended to spout it, with learned references to sections and subsections. It was exhilarating, too, to discover that we actually knew more about the law than the lawyers did, but this in itself was of small help to the old person who wanted to know how to set about collecting "the social security." The terminology itself was confusing; I doubt that the public in general has ever come to distinguish between such terms as welfare, assistance, benefits, insurance, compensation, although these words had precise legal meanings and little in common. The philosophy underlying these distinctions, of which much was made by the framers of the programs, held that Americans over age sixty-five would support a plan for "insurance benefits" based on the varying previous earnings of the individual, and turn proudly away from "welfare" or "assistance" payments based on need and presumably on destitution. What this becomes in the insurance program is to pay A $91.60 as a monthly benefit, for example, and by dint of prodigious record-keeping carried on at an astronomical cost, to pay B $91.85, or $94.02, on the grounds that B's records show more earnings. The practical effects of such differences are certainly debatable, while most of the old people that I know who really need the "insurance benefit" are by no means disdainful of "assistance" into the bargain, especially in those states where old-age assistance is often large enough to make the insurance payments seem niggardly. To explain why the social security programs in general need profound revision would be a book-length job, so I shall say only that they were created to meet conditions that have long ceased to exist and they have little to do with what such legislation, in the light of past experience, would be for today's needs and those of the future.

Foremost among problems as our work began to take form

245

was the presidential campaign of 1936, when any administrative move by the board touched off Republican objections on a grand scale. The post offices were about to issue the application forms for social security account numbers, and this was seized upon as a scheme to make every American wear a "dog tag" on a chain around his neck. I remember being shocked by what I regarded as an all but criminal falsehood: the papers carried photographs of a man wearing only shorts, and it was either Alf Landon, the candidate, or John D. M. Hamilton, the chairman of the Republican National Committee, who was pointing to the telltale chain and tag around the man's neck. The implication was not only that we were going to make him wear the tag but that we would make him take his clothes off to prove it. Why, as a newspaperman who thought himself highly informed on the ways of politics, I should have been so surprised by these tactics is hard for me to understand today. We actually sought reassurance from Washington and were relieved to learn that no dog tags were to be used, and it was hardly conceivable to me that the candidate himself, and his most highly placed advisers, would indulge in such fabrications.

I was laboring, once again, under the same naïveté that had made me astonished to find that the senator's mistress had been cleared by the Civil Service Commission as an "expert" informational officer. I was too green to realize that the dog-tag allegation was not so farfetched as it seemed, since we were in fact laying out the first steps in fastening a lifelong number on the individual. Most of all, I was too green to know, offhand, that the whole episode would be ignored by the electorate in its determination not to replace its hero F.D.R. with the nonentity governor of Kansas. I took it very seriously, as it seems to me I took everything, great and small, during my sojourn in the classified Civil Service of the United States.

I suppose much of this seriousness, not to say worry, about our work resulted from the general climate with which the press surrounded the New Deal, its "professors," and what it chose to regard as a kind of jocular insanity on the part of the President, its creator. By 1936, at the peak of his popularity, newspaper proprietors had turned bitterly against him; their staffs had seen too many of their own people dumped into the void of unemployment to feel quite the same way; the news and editorial writers, consequently, were disposed to go along with such programs as ours, and we were getting powerful support from many papers that denounced the Administration regularly on other counts. If we could only avoid some wild lapse or folly in our dealings with the press and the public, there was much solid informational work that our field organization—rapidly becoming a big one, with some fifty offices planned for New England and more later—could accomplish.

Washington was not long in giving us something fancy to worry about. It must have been some time in October when the office boy unloaded on my office table 100 or more, perhaps 200, cartons from a large packing box. Each contained a reel of 35-millimeter movie film, and since we had no word of what they were for or why, we left them on the table.

A few days later came a long memorandum: we were to book the films without charge—one reel dealing with old-age insurance, and another telling about the other parts of the program—into any theaters that would show them. There were great bundles of forms for us and the theater to fill in, mailing labels, shipping instructions; I believe there was even some prescribed action (with forms) for us to take against a theater that failed to return the reels. We had no practical way of finding out whether the films were actually shown by the theaters, but like "informational interview," the goal was partly statistical, and we were not disposed to look behind what the theaters told us.

Few activities draw so sharp a line between the dabbler and the professional as the production of motion-picture film. Regardless of subject matter, the effective use of the sound film is simply unattainable by beginners; compared with their efforts, the cheapest, shoddiest quickie from Hollywood is a model of suave storytelling and technical excellence. In a documentary, the difference is even more pronounced: here the bungler's best becomes a hodgepodge of pictorial propositions, poorly connected if at all, the narration often unrelated to the pictures, and the whole managing to ramble and to make its eventual point almost as an afterthought.

This simple lesson became painfully clear to John Pearson and me as we sat with the proprietor of a chain of New England theaters in his projection room, watching the board's two documentaries. I wonder whether any reel of these two productions survives today in the archives, for they would be worth reviewing: a mixture of stilted interviews with people whom I knew as perfectly civilized and sensible, but who were made to seem self-important, didactic, and even untidy in their appearance. Their pronouncements were punctuated by crude animated cartoons in which merry streams of dollars came hopping and skipping out of the U. S. Treasury and right into the pocket —perhaps it was the bank account—of Mr. John Q. Citizen. Something for nothing, in spite of all our indoctrination to the contrary, was the order of the day; Uncle Handout would soon be pelting the public with money.

The films, in spite of their exaggerative implications of easy money to come, were so amateurishly contrived that one could scarcely imagine what a theater audience could make of them. Some of their statements were incorrect. Persons with a near-term stake in the programs would inevitably be disappointed if they believed the films, and everyone else, it seemed to us, would find them unintelligible and boring.

The owner of the theater chain turned to us sympathetically as the showing ended and the lights went on. "Really tough, aren't they," he remarked. He genially agreed, nevertheless, to show them in his theaters. We thanked him and were about to take our leave. "By the way," said the theater man, "where are you storing these films?" I told him they were stacked on my office table.

"In your *office?*" The theater man was shocked. "My god!" he said. "How long have they been there?" I am sure he had rightly sized us up at being generally ignorant of the film business, but he was genuinely alarmed on finding out how grossly he had underestimated our ignorance. "My god," he said, "these films ought to be in a vault. They could burn the building down and kill a lot of people." He hastened to explain: What we had were nitrate, not safety, films. They could be used only in a fireproof projection booth by a licensed operator. They were highly combustible and given to blowing up for no particular reason other than a jolt or a supposedly moderate rise in temperature. I recalled that a few nitrate films that a man was carrying in a suitcase had exploded in a car of the Boylston Street subway a few years earlier and all but melted the whole car, so intense was the heat, and that several passengers had lost their lives.

The films, piled high on my office table, would have remained there until they finally blew up, I assume, so far as Washington was concerned. Our telephone calls and warnings made no impression: we were not authorized to rent a vault for the films, and that was that. But a three-holiday weekend was imminent, and John Pearson decided that none of us could enjoy it so long as the films were allowed to stay on the table. He telephoned one of the film companies, arranged for the proper storage, and the films were off our hands that afternoon.

We were glad that the films could not be used except in the fireproof booth, for this ruled them out on all sorts of occasions when we should have been obliged to show them, and they were not films that we wanted to show to anyone. Our Henry

Thurston persuaded Washington, eventually, to pay the storage bill.

Working for the government was not only a splendid refuge for one escaping from the *Transcript* but also an extraordinarily interesting interval, filled with many novelties, especially so for one unaccustomed to being part of an organization-chart way of life on the grand scale. The first three years of it were exciting and challenging, but once the beginnings had been made and the new programs more or less stabilized the repetition—on the grand scale—become tedious. After five years of it I was in a dead end, I decided, and perhaps good for one more move, provided I could find the escape hatch.

The hatch in this case led to the *Atlantic,* where I went to work after resigning from the government service. My first day at the *Atlantic* was a long one; I worked with great intensity. But when I set out for home that evening I felt anything but fatigued. I felt so vigorous, stimulated, yet curiously at ease that I could not help wondering why. What had happened during the day to give me such a lift?

The answer came to me abruptly: no report to write, no need, in so small and intimately associated a group as ours, to write the day up and prove that I had been there and done a day's work. In fact, all I had to do was my work, and never again in my occupational life was I to write another report.

Epilogue

Louis M. Lyons was on the staff of *The Boston Globe* while I was working on the *Transcript*. We found ourselves together on many occasions, and he was one of our most valued friends. He became curator of the Nieman Foundation at Harvard while I was working for the government, and I was sitting next to him at a seminar one day, late in 1940, for which I had provided a Washington functionary as speaker. It was all very pleasant and lively.

"By the way," said Louis, "do you know anyone who wants a job on the *Atlantic Monthly?*" I asked him what sort of job.

"It would be some kind of editorial work. Edward Weeks, you know, has succeeded Ellery Sedgwick as the editor, but the rest of the staff is mostly women. I believe they pay very little."

It sounded anything but exciting. No, I said, I knew no one, offhand, who might fit into it. I thought no more about the conversation for a week or so. But I was bored and stalled in the job with the Social Security Board. Unless we moved to Washington or New York, the prospects for any great increase in my status were poor. I was forty-one, nearing forty-two and I did not feel like settling for what I had: a reasonably secure minor position in the government service. One night, quite late, I recalled the conversation and telephoned Louis.

Louis seemed astonished that I should be interested in the job. "You mean for yourself?" he asked. "Well, I'll call Weeks the first thing tomorrow and tell him so."

Weeks telephoned me the next morning and invited me to lunch. In all the time I had been in Boston, I had never met him nor had any dealings of any sort with the *Atlantic*. We both belonged to the St. Botolph Club, which occupied a spacious and ruinous old building on what later became the parking lot of the Ritz Carlton, when the club moved to a location on Commonwealth Avenue, but Weeks and I knew each other not at all. With him to lunch at the Botolph came Donald Snyder, publisher and treasurer of the *Atlantic*. They were both likable and stimulating company, and we fell into a discussion of the magazine, the government, books, and politics. Nothing was said about the job at the *Atlantic* and we parted as if it had been sociability and no more that brought us together.

I remember only one other trifle from that occasion: as I was leaving the club, after Weeks and Snyder had gone, I picked up just outside at the curb a nickel. It seemed to me a good omen, but as weeks and months went by without the least further word from Weeks, I began to doubt it. I saw him from time to time at the club, and we exchanged greetings, but it did seem to me that he owed me at least some minimal notice that he was filling the job with some other candidate, which I concluded he had long since done.

It was a Saturday morning in February, 1941, when I had a telephone call from Weeks at my office. "Charlie," he began breezily, "we have been looking over various people for the job at the *Atlantic* and I'm happy to tell you that you are elected for it. Could you begin on Monday?"

I said I did not think I could wind up my government affairs that quickly, but that I could begin in about six weeks. We sat down at the Botolph together that Sunday afternoon and quickly came to an agreement. The starting salary was not at all what I needed, but I was sure that it was the right place for me. Much better days would come, I thought, and they did. The quarter-century from that time to this was all that I could have wished it to be. There was never a moment in it when I would have changed places with anyone, anywhere.